I0199825

P. T. FORSYTH
BIBLIOGRAPHY
AND INDEX

Recent Titles in
Bibliographies and Indexes in Religious Studies

P. T. FORSYTH BIBLIOGRAPHY AND INDEX

Robert Benedetto

Foreword by Donald G. Miller

Bibliographies and Indexes in Religious Studies,
Number 27

Greenwood Press

WESTPORT, CONNECTICUT • LONDON

Library of Congress Cataloging-in-Publication Data

Benedetto, Robert.
    P.T. Forsyth bibliography and index / Robert Benedetto ; foreword
by Donald G. Miller.
      p.   cm.—(Bibliographies and indexes in religious studies,
ISSN 0742-6836 ; no. 27)
    ISBN 0-313-28753-8 (alk. paper)
    1. Forsyth, Peter Taylor, 1848-1921—Bibliography. 2. Forsyth,
Peter Taylor, 1848-1921—Indexes.   I. Title. II. Series.
Z8309.4.B46 1993
[BX7260.F583]
016.230'58'092—dc20   92-46527

British Library Cataloguing in Publication Data is available.

Copyright © 1993 by Robert Benedetto

All rights reserved. No portion of this book may be
reproduced, by any process or technique, without the
express written consent of the publisher.

Library of Congress Catalog Card Number: 92-46527
ISBN: 0-313-28753-8
ISSN: 0742-6836

First published in 1993

Greenwood Press, 88 Post Road West, Westport, CT 06881
An imprint of Greenwood Publishing Group, Inc.

Printed in the United States of America

∞

The paper used in this book complies with the
Permanent Paper Standard issued by the National
Information Standards Organization (Z39.48-1984).

10 9 8 7 6 5 4 3 2 1

To

DIKRAN Y. HADIDIAN

Librarian Emeritus
Pittsburgh Theological Seminary
Pittsburgh, Pennsylvania

CONTENTS

II. Source Index for Principal Works

FOREWORD

Anything that helps to make the thought of P. T. Forsyth more easily available is a service of inestimable value to the theological world and to the life of the church. Forsyth had an unusually fertile and creative mind, along with an intuitive grasp of the Christian faith which led him into depths of understanding which are not given to many.

There was in him a combination of intellectual power and devotional fire that made his thoughts live. The contours of his mind were shaped in the white heat of wrestling prayer. The religious sentiments of his heart were formed and controlled by sustained and rigorous mental discipline.

Although a convinced Congregationalist, he had risen above all petty and hampering denominationalism and was truly catholic in outlook. His theological thought bristled with life, for he tested it constantly in the home, in pulpit and parish, and in relation to the arts and science and philosophies of his day, and against the social and political problems then current.

Forsyth had an uncanny capacity to analyze the trends of his time, both secular and churchly, separating the wheat from the chaff; distinguishing between the truly new and the merely novel; knowing the difference between a healthy respect for tradition and a crippling antiquarianism, between authority and authoritarianism, between genuine creativity and dilettantism, between genuine critical study of the Bible which helped to span the distance between the world of the Scriptures and the modern age, and the stultifying biblical criticism which robbed the Bible of its transcendent message and turned it into a vehicle of current humanism.

He had a broad knowledge of classical thought, of art and literature, both ancient and modern, of philosophy and science, and used the biblical message to enrich the genuine contributions of these fields to human thought and endeavor, and to judge their limitations, biases, and weaknesses.

He was, as all are, a theologian of his time, yet was a theologian for all times, with insights that will abide the shifting impulses of the generations. He was, and will continue to be, a theologian who though at times bypassed and forgotten (because he tells us what we do not want to hear) will be rediscovered in the crises of life. His relevance, although superficially shaped in the thought struggles of his time, is timeless. One scholar remarked that the best book on the Second World War was written by Forsyth during the First World War.

There was no narrowness in him; he covered a broad spectrum of subjects. There are few areas of Christian thought on which he did not leave a deposit of worthy comment.

Forsyth, nevertheless, had a tantalizing way of writing. His books are almost totally without footnotes. He often refers to Scripture passages without identifying them. His references to other scholars are often imprecise in wording, and difficult to locate in their writings. Most of his works are without indices.

One glance at this *Bibliography and Index* will serve as a testimony to the diligence and skill of its author. The labors here represented are herculean. The information is both detailed and exhaustive, and so arranged that one can locate without effort the titles of all Forsyth's writings, the subject matter covered, the authors cited and the titles of their works, along with the location of the passages quoted, and all the Scripture passages Forsyth discussed. It is a veritable gold mine of information, and should prove to be a major milestone in Forsyth research.

The entire theological world is greatly indebted to the author, who abundantly merits our gratitude.

Donald G. Miller

PREFACE

The Bibliography. The theological literature of the past seventy years reflects a steady interest in the theology of P. T. Forsyth, demonstrated by the preparation of seventeen dissertations, and the publication of a continuous stream of books and articles. Despite this continued interest, no comprehensive Forsyth bibliography has ever been published. In 1949, William L. Bradley prepared an excellent list of Forsyth's articles and contemporary newspaper reports about his career, but the bibliography was omitted by Independent Press when his dissertation was published in 1952. As a result, Bradley's list remained locked away in the dissertation format for thirty-two years.[1] In 1981, the present writer was asked to prepare a bibliography for a new edition of *Positive Preaching and Modern Mind*. At that time, the Bradley material was incorporated into the bibliography and finally published.[2]

The 1981 bibliography, which contained 557 entries, was never intended to be exhaustive. Since that time, the list has been expanded to 772 entries and revised and corrected. Three additional improvements have been made: 1) the format of the bibliography has been improved and a numbering system added to help locate specific titles, 2) editions and reprintings of Forsyth's books have now been included and, following Bradley's example, reprintings of journal articles or revisions of articles which were incorporated into other publications, are identified, and 3) a new name index has been prepared to complement the revised title index of Forsyth's writings. As with the original title index, book titles appear in capital letters while articles appear in regular type; the numbers which follow refer to the numbered item(s), not page numbers.

This new bibliography now brings together all materials listed in the standard library catalogs, periodical indexes, and databases in the United States and Britain. While the bibliography has been compiled with a view toward comprehensiveness, it has not been possible to identify all of Forsyth's articles and pamphlets. The exact number of these materials is unknown, but scholars have estimated that Forsyth published between 260-280 articles and nearly 50 pamphlets.[3] Many of the articles remain buried in unindexed newspapers and magazines, while some of the pamphlets may remain in uncataloged collections. To complicate matters, Forsyth used at least one pseudonym, "Publicola," and is known to have published material in *The Manchester Examiner and Times* under that name between 1885 and 1889. While a few of these articles have been discovered and included herein, others may still await discovery since the newspaper must be searched by hand for unknown material. Also, Forsyth's newspaper articles sometimes appear under the byline, "From a Nonconformist Correspondent." With such a designation, of course, it is extremely difficult to identify Forsyth's work. With these considerable limitations in mind, the bibliography is now offered as an authoritative list.

The bibliography is divided into two parts: publications by Forsyth and literature about Forsyth. Each part is subdivided by type of material (anthologies and collections, books, contributions to books, etc.), these types being arranged in alphabetical order. The material in each subdivision of part one is listed in chronological order, except for the citations under "Anthologies and Collections," which are listed alphabetically by author. The material in each subdivision of part two is listed in alphabetical order with two exceptions: 1) the citations under "Reports in Newspapers" are arranged alphabetically by newspaper title and then chronologically, 2) "Reviews of Books and Articles" is subdivided into "Reviews of Forsyth's Publications" and "Reviews of Publications about Forsyth," the citations under both subdivisions being arranged in alphabetical order by title, and then alphabetically by the title of the journal in which the review appeared.

The Source Index. All of Forsyth's books, with the exception of *The Principle of Authority* lack indices. For many students and scholars, this omission has become a barrier to both the casual enjoyment and serious use of Forsyth's publications. To help alleviate this problem, source indices have been prepared to the major works themselves. A close study of these sources may yield new information about the development of Forsyth's theology. Forsyth's citation of German philosophers and theologians, and English poets is well-known. Less well-known is his remark that in the quest for truth one moves through philosophy and poetry to revelation.[4] Forsyth's works resound with this interaction and movement and his citations reflect the warp and woof of his mind. However, in any study of these sources one should remember, as William Bradley said and Donald Miller reminds us: Forsyth is more than the sum of his sources; "he produced something distinctively his own."[5]

Because there is no "critical text" of Forsyth's works, the indexing is based, with a few exceptions, on the older British editions published by Hodder & Stoughton between 1899-1915 and the modern editions published by Independent Press between 1938 and 1962. (See the list of Abbreviations on pages xvii and xviii for the specific editions which have been indexed.) Many of these editions have also been reprinted in the United States, and the bibliography may be checked in order to identify these reprintings. Forsyth's books are also widely available from university and seminary libraries via interlibrary loan. Because many books are now becoming very brittle with age, some microfiche editions are beginning to appear.

The complete texts of Forsyth's major books, including his prefaces, addenda and bibliographies have been indexed. Prefaces or introductory materials prepared by others have not been indexed. Also, chapter eight in *The Church and the Sacraments*, "The Place of the Sacraments in the Teaching of St. Paul," was written by Forsyth's colleague, Herbert T. Andrews. While this chapter is indexed in order to maintain the continuity of argument in the book, readers should be aware that the citations are not Forsyth's.

The "Source Index for Principal Works" consists of three indices: a cumulative Scripture Index, a cumulative Index of Names and Cited Works, and individual scripture and name indices for each of Forsyth's books. These separate book indices also include the table of contents of each indexed work. These contents pages will help the reader identify the specific chapters in which citations appear and will enable comparisons with other editions of the same work which may have different pagination.

The Scripture Index includes both identified and unidentified scriptural references. Since many of Forsyth's quotations are paraphrased, the index will help to identify specific texts as well as patterns of citation. The Index of Names includes authors, artists, musicians, and other persons mentioned by Forsyth. While persons from classical and biblical times are also included, Greek gods and literary and other fictional characters are excluded. The index also includes references to books and periodical articles, to specific plays and poems, and to musical and artistic works cited in the texts. Many unidentified or partially identified names and references have now been fully identified, but several unidentified poetic quotations have eluded the indexer. It is probable that several of these elusive quotations are from poets and authors cited elsewhere, rather than from completely new sources.

Acknowledgements. I am especially indebted to William L. Bradley for his early work on the journal literature. His identification of most of Forsyth's published articles is the real heart of the bibliography. Several other Forsyth scholars have contributed to this project over the years, including the late Charles S. Duthie, Principal of New College, University of London; Clifford S. Pitt, Academic Dean of Miles College in Birmingham, Alabama; and Rev. Thomas D. Meadley. These scholars supplied information or substantial lists which have been incorporated in the present work. Although the resources of many libraries were utilized, The British Library Newspaper Library was particularly helpful. Patsy Verrault, Reference Librarian at Union Theological Seminary in Virginia provided valuable reference assistance and helped to arrange interlibrary loans. Martha L. Moore-Keish, my student assistant during the 1991-1992 academic year, verified numerous citations, compiled the name index for the bibliography, and helped to prepare the material for publication. I am also grateful to Donald G. Miller, President Emeritus of Pittsburgh Theological Seminary in Pittsburgh, Pennsylvania, for introducing this work.

Finally, a large debt is owed to Dikran Y. Hadidian of Pickwick Publications who commissioned the 1981 bibliography and gave permission to incorporate herein materials from that earlier edition. I am also grateful for Hadidian's *Bibliography of British Theological Literature, 1850-1940*[6] which was frequently consulted in the preparation of the name indices. To this librarian, publisher, and longtime student of British theological literature, this book is gratefully and respectfully dedicated.

NOTES

[1] W. L. Bradley, *The Theology of P. T. Forsyth, 1848-1921* (Ph.D. thesis, University of Edinburgh, 1949).

[2] In Donald G. Miller, Browne Barr, and Robert S. Paul, *P. T. Forsyth; The Man, the Preachers' Theologian: Prophet for the 20th Century: A Contemporary Assessment* (Pittsburgh: Pickwick Press, 1981), 73-112.

[3] Brown and Rodgers estimate the number of articles at "more than 260," while Miller puts the total at "about 280" and "almost 50 pamphlets." See Robert M. Brown, *P. T. Forsyth, Prophet for Today* (Philadelphia: Westminster Press, 1952), 171; John H. Rodgers, *The Theology of P. T. Forsyth: The Cross of Christ and the Revelation of God* (London: Independent Press, 1965), 9; Donald K. McKim, ed., *Encyclopedia of the Reformed Faith* (Louisville, Kentucky: Westminster/John Knox Press, 1992), s.v. "Forsyth, Peter Taylor," by Donald G. Miller, 142.

[4] *The Justification of God* (London: Latimer House Limited, 1948), 134-135.

[5] Donald G. Miller, "P. T. Forsyth: The Man," in Miller, Barr, and Paul, *P. T. Forsyth; The Man, the Preachers' Theologian*, 22. For a brief discussion of Forsyth's sources see Harry Escott, *The Cure of Souls: An Anthology of P. T. Forsyth's Practical Writings*, rev. and enl. ed. (Grand Rapids: William B. Eerdmans, 1971), 7-17.

[6] (Pittsburgh: The Clifford E. Barbour Library, Pittsburgh Theological Seminary, 1985).

ABBREVIATIONS

CAS   The Church and the Sacraments, [3d. ed.]. London: Independent Press, 1949.

CAR   Congregationalism and Reunion. London: Independent Press, 1952. Containing: "Reunion and Recognition" (CAR-RR) and "Congregationalism and Reunion" (CAR-CR).

CEW   The Christian Ethic of War. London: Longmans, Green, and Co., 1916.

CGS   The Church, the Gospel and Society. London: Independent Press, 1962. Containing: "A Holy Church the Moral Guide of Society," 1905 (CGS-HC); and "The Grace of the Gospel as the Moral Authority in the Church," 1905 (CGS-GG).

COP   Christ on Parnassus, 2nd. ed. London: Independent Press, 1959.

COC   The Charter of the Church. London: Alexander and Shepheard, 1896.

COTC   The Cruciality of the Cross, 2nd. ed. London: Independent Press, 1948.

FFF   Faith, Freedom and the Future, 2nd. ed. London: Independent Press, 1955.

GHF   God the Holy Father. London: Independent Press, 1957. Containing: The Holy Father and the Living Christ, 1897 (GHF-HFLC); Christian Perfection, 1899 (GHF-CP); and The Taste of Death and the Life of Grace, 1901 (GHF-TDLG).

JOG   Justification of God, [2nd. ed.]. London: Independent Press, 1948.

MER   Marriage; Its Ethic and Religion. London: Hodder & Stoughton, 1912.

MSC   Missions in State and Church. London: Hodder & Stoughton, 1908.

POA   Principal of Authority, 2nd. ed. London: Independent Press, 1952.

PPJC   Person and Place of Jesus Christ. London: Independent Press, 1948.

PPMM   Positive Preaching and the Modern Mind, 3rd. ed. London: Independent Press, 1949.

RRR   Rome, Reform and Reaction. London: Hodder & Stoughton, 1899.

RRA   Religion in Recent Art, 3rd. ed. London: Hodder & Stoughton, 1905.

SCP   Socialism, the Church and the Poor. London: Hodder & Stoughton, 1908.

SOP   The Soul of Prayer, [2nd. ed.]. London: Independent Press, 1949.

TCS   Theology in Church and State. London: Hodder & Stoughton, 1915.

TLTN   This Life and the Next, [2nd. ed.]. London: Independent Press, 1946.

WOC   The Work of Christ, 2nd. ed. London: Independent Press, 1938.

INTRODUCTION

P. T. Forsyth was born in Aberdeen, Scotland, on 12 May 1848. His mother, Elspet MacPherson Forsyth, worked as a housemaid for more than nine years in the home of Peter Taylor, a prominent merchant, member of the town council, and one of the founders of Blackfriars Street Congregational Church. When Taylor died he bequeathed his sixteen-room house to the Forsyths who named their first son after him. Forsyth's father, Isaac, worked for a time as a bookseller and then became employed in the post office, while his mother took in student boarders and raised five children. In spite of their hard work, the Forsyths remained very poor and their son suffered through bouts of sickness. The Forsyths became members of the Blackfriars Street Church (now Skene Street Congregational Church), which achieved some notoriety for sending missionaries to China. The church was also a gathering place for university students and intellectuals under the leadership of John Kennedy (1836-1846) and Joseph Vickery (1871-1882). It was here that Forsyth received his first religious instruction and became involved in the large, well-run junior program of the church.

Educated at the local parish school and Grammar School, Forsyth entered Aberdeen University in 1864. At Aberdeen he studied classics and philosophy and was taught by professors Ramsay, William Minto, William Hunter, and Alexander Bain. It was here that he read George Elliot, Carlyle, Ruskin, Wordsworth and other luminaries who would leave a marked impression upon his thinking. He also developed a strong interest in art and music which he maintained throughout his life. After graduating with first class honors and a gold medal in 1869, he worked as an assistant in classics to Professor Black of Kings College, Aberdeen, and as a private tutor in the home of Patrick Davidson. On the advice of William Robertson Smith, a friend and fellow graduate one or two years his senior who had studied in Germany, Forsyth spent a term at Göttingen where he learned German and attended the lectures of Albrecht Ritschl. Forsyth's study in Germany was a life-changing experience which would affect all of his subsequent work. In 1872 he returned to Britain and enrolled in New College, Hampstead, where he studied theology and embraced the works of F. D. Maurice, whom Smith had also recommended. However, poor health prevented him from regularly attending lectures and he gradually became dissatisfied with the school's theological program. In 1874, he withdrew without completing the course of study.

While at New College, Forsyth became a member of Baldwin Brown's congregation at Brixton in south London. Brown, also a disciple of Maurice, helped Forsyth secure his first pastorate at the Congregational Church in Shipley, Yorkshire, a suburb of Bradley, in 1876. Forsyth then began a twenty-five year career in the Congregational ministry serving four urban and one university church: Shipley, 1876-1880; St. Thomas'-Square Church, Hackney, a suburb of London, 1880-1885; Cheetham Hill, in north Manchester, 1885-1888; Clarendon Park, Leicester, 1888-1894; and Emmanuel Church, Cambridge, 1894-1901. Forsyth developed into an inspiring, if lengthy, preacher, gifted in the use of language and able to move an audience with a vigorous presentation of the gospel message. While in the pastorate, he also developed an interest in politics and was deeply involved in the social questions of his time.

In 1877 Forsyth married Minna Magness, a warm, cultured person whose serene disposition contrasted sharply with that of her highly-strung, somewhat impatient husband. The Forsyths had a daughter, Jessie Forsyth Andrews. Following Minna's death in 1891, Forsyth, already ill from six years of overwork at Clarendon Park, entered a three-year period in which he suffered from nervous exhaustion. It wasn't until his remarriage to Bertha Ison in 1898 that he began to regain his former strength. His last years at Emmanuel Church, surrounded by students, colleagues, and family, were very rewarding.

With improved health, Forsyth began two decades of vigorous activity. In 1901 he accepted the principalship of Hackney College, London (later renamed New College), a theological college newly recognized by the University of London. In addition to his administrative duties, which included lengthy business committee meetings and burdensome fund-raising for the financially-ailing school, Forsyth taught and counseled students, spoke at numerous churches on behalf of the college, and traveled to Boston in 1899 where he addressed the International Congregational Council, and to Yale University in 1907 where he gave the Lyman Beecher Lecture on Preaching. He also became a reluctant disputant with R. J. Campbell concerning the "New Theology" which he considered a grave danger to the church. In 1910 he assumed additional responsibilities by becoming dean of the Faculty of Theology at the University of London. However, the outbreak of World War I interrupted the academic life of both Hackney College and the university. The college was eventually commandeered by the British government and Forsyth began to devote more time to writing, producing six books in four years. Honored by Aberdeen University with a Doctor of Divinity degree in 1895, Forsyth also served as president of the Congregational Union of England and Wales in 1905. Forsyth remained at Hackney College until 1920, where, following a year of declining health, he died at age seventy-three on 11 November 1921.[1]

Forsyth began his pastoral career as a liberal in the tradition of Albrecht Ritschl. He was deeply absorbed in biblical criticism and was invited to attend the now infamous Leicester Conference in 1877, a gathering convened by a group of Congregational ministers who many considered to be left wing, if not heretical. However, as the young minister came face-to-face with the physical and spiritual needs of his largely working-class congregations, he gradually began to question his own theological views. The academic, "ivory tower" liberalism in which he was trained made him ill-equipped to deal with the harsh realities of nineteenth century industrial Britain. He also experienced a change of heart, wherein the gospel came to him in a personal way. In an often-quoted biographical passage Forsyth tells us, "Whereas I first thought that what the churches needed was enlightened instruction and liberal theology, I came to be sure that what they needed was evangelization, in something more than the conventional sense of that word."[2] Forsyth's "conversion" was both a significant period of intellectual reappraisal as well as a new experience of faith. Thereafter, he would characterize the old liberalism as an extreme theological position and consider it a spent theological movement.[3]

Although Forsyth became an outspoken critic of nineteenth century liberalism, he was no mere reactionary. His theological work contains no longing for the old orthodoxy of the past, but proclaims instead a new, Christ-centered theology based on the modern, critical study of the Scriptures. His own views were prodigiously set forth in twenty-five books, more than 260 articles, and other publications. He is best known for his six major works: *Positive Preaching and Modern Mind* (1907), the Yale lectures on preaching; *The Person and Place of Jesus Christ* (1909), an extremely important book on the subject of Christology, and his greatest work; *The Work of Christ* (1910), which contains insights on the atonement; *The Principle of Authority* (1912), a difficult book on the philosophy of religion; *The Justification of God* (1916), on evil and the history of redemption, an important theodicy, and; *The Church and the Sacraments* (1917), on the nature of the church, baptism and the Lord's supper.[4] Among Forsyth's lesser-known works are his books on art and theology, *Religion in Recent Art* (1887) and *Christ on Parnassus* (1911); a book on prayer, *The Soul of Prayer* (1916); an important work written in light of World War I which supports "just war," *The Christian Ethic of War* (1917); and his last theological work, *This Life and the Next* (1918), subtitled, "The Effect on This Life of Faith in Another."

In Forsyth's earlier writings one can see the obvious influence of F. D. Maurice to whom he owed much. He was also well-read in Hegel, Martin Kähler and Kierkegaard, had great command of English poetry and literature, and kept abreast of contemporary German theology. He especially appreciated German dogmatic works, including the books of Friedrich Loofs, D. M. Reischle and Theodore Kaftan. Of primary importance was the theology of his teacher, Albrecht Ritschl, who rejected mysticism, rationalism, creedal orthodoxy, and metaphysics in theology; emphasized the primacy of faith; insisted that the gospel was given to the community of faith, rather than to individuals; and believed that morality was the heart of the Christian life. Forsyth believed in the preeminence of German scholarship and felt that no comparable theological works had been written in the English language. However, he did praise the work of American William Adams Brown and two British contemporaries R. W. Dale and James Denney.

From the time of his break with liberalism in 1894, Forsyth also came to appreciate the Puritan divines and Calvin, so that his later work became less dependent upon Ritschl. He also turned to St. Paul, where he found a Christ-centered and cross-centered theology. While many contemporaries were still proclaiming the "love of God," Forsyth began to write and lecture about a "holy God," and then about sin, judgement and reconciliation. It is quite remarkable that in 1910 while the young Karl Barth (still under the liberal spell of his teacher Wilhelm Herrmann, also a Ritschlian) was writing an essay on "The Christian Faith in History" in which he made "the experience of the individual" the basis of faith, Forsyth was writing of the "Christ for us," to describe a God-centered, rather than man-centered theology.[5] For this reason, Forsyth has been called a pre-Barthian or the "Barth" before Barth.[6] But Forsyth is not so easily categorized; he is neither a classic liberal nor a neoorthodox theologian and should be considered independent of both schools of thought. He was an original thinker who some consider a prophet of our times.[7]

Even the books of a "prophet" are subject to criticism, and Forsyth's work has certainly received its share. Some find his obscure language particularly bothersome. His writings contain many passages where new words are coined or where the language is difficult to interpret and thus the meaning is left in doubt. He was particularly fond of antithesis and epigram. Others object to his repetitiveness of style ("in page after page in his books we seem to be reading exercises in language; the thought makes no progress"[8]) and substance (continual references to the atonement theme). Some have also lamented the fact that while his books on the atonement are extremely perceptive and valuable, he never really covers the ground in an exhaustive way so that they are inadequate as dogmatic works. While these and other criticisms are partly justified, they should not deter modern readers from experiencing Forsyth's great literary prose or pondering some of the best theological writing of the modern era. We only need to turn to Forsyth's great chapter, "The Plerosis or the Self-Fulfillment of Christ," in *The Person and Place of Jesus Christ*, or to "The Moral Poignancy of the Cross" in *Positive Preaching and the Modern Mind* to realize that this is great theological writing which presses the limits of language and leaves us with the ultimate paradoxes of faith. Theological writing cannot do more than this.

Forsyth also leaves us with a legacy of good judgement drawn from years of biblical study. Several points come to mind. First, he recognized the importance of modern biblical scholarship and weighed carefully its findings. He had little patience for those who dismissed textual study as simply an attack on "holy writ." Rather, he viewed such study as allied with the purpose of expounding the message of the scriptures in a modern, truthful and constructive manor. Second, as a theologian he was very concerned about the dogmatic underpinnings of the gospel. He rejected theological systems based on the centrality of man, arguing from the Pauline model that biblical theology is a God-centered, cross-centered theology. Third, he came to reject both liberalism and fundamentalism as theological extremes which involved a significant distortion of the biblical message. He sought to forge a middle way which would embrace "liberal" studies, yet preserve the ancient, Christ-centered gospel. Fourth, Forsyth was very concerned about the life of the church. He tried to revive the preached word and stressed both the personal and corporate importance of the sacraments. And, he strongly linked the church with the gospel. "The church," he said, "is where that gospel is."[9] Without the gospel there is simply no church. He also tried to promote church unity which, as he envisioned, was not achieved through denominational mergers, but through the organization of a federated community; a "united states of the church." And finally, in all of his work, he sought to "ethicize" the gospel by bringing the biblical message into the conscience and morality into the world. To Forsyth, the gospel was not abstract truth, but a relationship which is lived out in a personal way, with both personal and social implications.

NOTES

[1]Several memorial sketches of Forsyth's life and thought, prepared by contemporaries, were published in the *British Weekly*, 17 November 1921. These include: W. Robertson Nicoll, "Principal Forsyth," 145-146; "Principal Forsyth: A Memoir, by One Who Knew Him," 162; J. K. Mozley, "A Personal Tribute," 162; and five other tributes. See also Jessie Forsyth Andrews, "Memoir," in P. T. Forsyth, *The Work of Christ*, 2d ed., (London: Independent Press, 1938), vii-xxviii.

[2]*Positive Preaching and the Modern Mind*, 2d ed. (London: Independent Press, 1949), 193.

[3]"That liberalism had its work to do. I felt its force. I took part in it. And it has won -- I might say all along the line. . . . But the result of the general victory of religious liberalism has been disappointing on the whole. . . . The movement was too sentimental. It interpreted the heavenly Fatherhood by the earthly, instead of the earthly by the heavenly. It was cowed by Huxley, and comforted by George MacDonald. Its ethic was more altruistic than evangelical, more of effort than of faith. . . . Its general

altruistic than evangelical, more of effort than of faith. . . . Its general
tendency was to canonize freedom instead of an authority that makes
free. . . . It is a spent movement." *The Examiner*, 5 November 1905, 462;
quoted in Robert McAfee Brown, *P. T. Forsyth: Prophet for Today*
(Philadelphia: The Westminster Press, 1952), 19.

[4]For the beginning student, the best introduction to these six books is
A. M. Hunter, *P. T. Forsyth* (Philadelphia: The Westminster Press, 1974).
For a more lengthy examination of Forsyth's writings see William L.
Bradley, *P. T. Forsyth, The Man and His Work* (London: Independent Press,
1952), 64-90.

[5]Claude Welch, *The Theology of Karl Barth*, audiotape lectures delivered
at Union Theological Seminary in Virginia, 1966; and *The Work of Christ*,
2d ed. (London: Independent Press, 1938), 130.

[6]T. Hywell Hughes, "A Barthian Before Barth?" *Congregational
Quarterly* 12 (July 1934): 308-315. Hughes sees areas of agreement between
Forsyth and Barth, but also substantial differences.

[7]Robert S. Paul, "Prophet for the Twentieth Century?," in Miller, Barr,
and Paul, *P. T. Forsyth; The Man, the Preachers' Theologian*, 42-68.

[8]W. Robertson Nicoll, "Principal Forsyth," *British Weekly* (17 November
1921)): 146.

[9]*The Church and the Sacraments* (London: Independent Press, 1947),
134.

I
P. T. FORSYTH
BIBLIOGRAPHY,
1886–1992

PUBLICATIONS OF P. T. FORSYTH

1. Anthologies and Collections

1.1   Anderson, Marvin W., ed. *The Gospel and Authority: A P. T. Forsyth Reader*. Minneapolis: Augsburg, 1971.

Contains eight articles published between 1905-1911 in the *Contemporary Review, Hibbert Journal*, and *London Quarterly Review*.

1.2   Escott, Harry. *The Cure of Souls: An Appraisement and Anthology of P. T. Forsyth's Practical Writings*. Rev. and enl. ed. London: George Allen and Unwin, 1971.

First published as *Peter Taylor Forsyth, 1848-1921, Director of Souls: Selections from His Practical Writings*. London: Epworth Press, 1948. Includes biographical and bibliographical notes, xvii-x.

1.3   Forsyth, P. T. *The Church, the Gospel and Society*. London: Independent Press, 1962.

Contains *A Holy Church the Moral Guide of Society* (1905) and *The Grace of the Gospel as the Moral Authority in the Church* (1905).

1.4   ———. *Congregationalism and Reunion, Two Lectures*. London: Independent Press, 1952.

Contains two lectures originally delivered in 1917 and 1918 titled "Reunion and Recognition" and "Congregationalism and Reunion."

1.5   ———. *God the Holy Father*. London: Independent Press, 1957.

Contains *The Holy Father and the Living Christ* (1897), *Christian Perfection* (1899), and *The Taste of Death and the Life of Grace* (1901). Reprinted by St. Andrews Press, Edinburgh, 1978.

1.6   Huxtable, John, ed. *Revelation Old and New: Sermons and Addresses*. London: Independent Press, 1962.

Contains nine sermons and addresses, several published in *The British Congregationalist* between 1906-1911; and four previously unpublished sermons: "Revelation Old and New," 1911; "The Ideal City," 1913; "The Church as the Corporate Missionary of the Gospel," 1909; and "Suffering," 1913.

1.7   Mikolaski, Samuel J., ed. *The Creative Theology of P. T. Forsyth; Selections from His Works*. Grand Rapids: Wm. B. Eerdmans, 1969.

Includes a selected bibliography, pp. 262-264.

2. Books

1886

2.1   *Pulpit Parables for Young Hearers*. With J. A. Hamilton. Manchester: Brook and Chrystal. viii, 227 pp.

1889

2.2   *Religion in Recent Art: Being Expository Lectures on Rossetti, Burne Jones, Watts, Holman Hunt, and Wagner*. Manchester: Abel Heywood and Son. x, 361 pp.

Editions:
    [2d ed.], Hodder & Stoughton, London, 1901. xii, 316 pp.
    3d ed., Hodder & Stoughton, London, 1905.
Microform editions:
    [2d ed.], Lost Cause Press, Louisville, 1975, 1976.
Reprintings:
    [1st ed.], Simpkin, Marshall and Co., London, 1889.
    [1st ed.], Hodder & Stoughton, London, 1899.
    [2d ed.], Hodder & Stoughton, London, 1902.
    [2d ed.], E. S. Gorham, New York, 1902.
    3d ed., Hodder & Stoughton, London, 1911.
    3d ed., AMS Press, New York, 1972.

1896

2.3   *The Charter of the Church: Six Lectures on the Spiritual Principle of Nonconformity*. London: Alexander and Shepheard. vi, 102 pp.

Microform editions:
    Alexander and Shepheard, London, 1990.

1897

2.4   *The Holy Father and the Living Christ*. Little Books on Religion. Edited by W. R. Nicoll. London: Hodder & Stoughton. 152 pp.

Reprinted in *God the Holy Father* (1957).

Microform editions:
    Hodder & Stoughton, London and New York, 1985.
Reprintings:
    Dodd, Mead & Company, New York, 1898, [1899].
    Hodder & Stoughton, London, 1900.
    Hodder & Stoughton, London, 1910, 1913.

1899

2.5   *Christian Perfection*. Little Books on Religion. Edited by W. R. Nicoll. London: Hodder & Stoughton. vii, 152 pp.

Reprinted in *God the Holy Father* (1957).

Editions:
    New ed., Hodder & Stoughton, London, 1909.
Microform editions:
    [1st ed.], Hodder & Stoughton, London and New York, 1989.
Reprintings:
    [1st ed.], Dodd, Mead & Company, New York, 1899.
    [New ed.], Hodder & Stoughton, London, [1913?].

2.6   *Rome, Reform and Reaction: Four Lectures on the Religious Situation*. London: Hodder & Stoughton. ix, 246 pp.

Microform editions:
    Historical Commission of the Southern Baptist Convention, Nashville, 1985.
    Hodder & Stoughton, London, 1985.

1901

2.7   *The Taste of Death and the Life of Grace*. Small Books on Great Subjects, 21. London: James Clarke. viii, 128 pp.

Reprinted in *God the Holy Father* (1957).

Editions:
    2d ed., James Clarke, London, 1906.

1907

2.8   *Positive Preaching and Modern Mind.* The Lyman Beecher Lectures
      on Preaching, Yale University. London: Hodder & Stoughton. xii,
      374 pp.

      Editions:
            2d ed., Hodder & Stoughton, London, 1909.
            [3d ed.], *Positive Preaching and the Modern Mind*,
            Independent Press, London, 1949. xi, 258 pp.
            1st American ed., Wm. B. Eerdmans, Grand Rapids, 1964.
            (Reprint of 3d ed.)
            2d American ed., *P. T. Forsyth–The Man, the Preacher's
            Theologian, Prophet for the 20th Century: A Contemporary
            Assessment*, Pickwick Press, Pittsburgh, 1981. (Contains
            reprint of 2d ed.)
      Reprintings:
            [1st ed.], Independent Press, London, 1907, 1960.
            [1st ed.], A. C. Armstrong & Son, New York, 1907, 1908.
            [1st ed.], Eaton & Mains, New York, 1907.
            [1st ed.], Jennings & Graham, Cincinnati, 1907.
            [1st ed.], A. C. Armstrong & Son, New York, 1908.
            [2d ed.], Hodder & Stoughton, London, 1914.
            [3d ed.], Independent Press, London, 1953, 1955, 1957, 1964.
            [3d ed.], Wm. B. Eerdmans, Grand Rapids, 1966.
            [1st ed.], Baker Book House, Grand Rapids, 1980. Notable
            Books on Preaching Series.
            [1st ed.], George H. Doran Co., New York, n.d.

1908

2.9   *Missions in State and Church. Sermons and Addresses.* London:
      Hodder & Stoughton. viii, 344 pp.

      Reprintings:
            A. C. Armstrong, New York, 1908.
            Jennings & Graham, Cincinnati, n.d.
            Eaton & Mains, New York, n.d.

2.10 *Socialism, the Church and the Poor.* London: Hodder & Stoughton.
      vii, 73 pp.

      The work consists of two parts: Part I: The Church and Socialism;
      Part II: Christ and the Poor. Part I appeared in substance in the
      British Congregationalist.

      Microform editions:
            Newberry Library, Chicago, 1968.

1909

2.11   *The Cruciality of the Cross.* The Expositor's Library. London: Hodder
& Stoughton. 226 pp.

The first two chapters of this book were first presented as the
opening address of the Third International Congregational Council
at Edinburgh in July 1908.

Editions:
2d ed., Independent Press, London, 1948. x, 104 pp.
Microform editions:
[1st ed.], Eaton & Mains, New York, 1985.
[1st ed.], Jennings & Graham, Cincinnati, 1985.
Reprintings:
[1st ed.], Eaton & Mains, New York, [1909].
[1st ed.], Jennings & Graham, Cincinnati, [1909].
[1st ed.], Hodder & Stoughton, London, 1910, 1914.
[2d ed.], Independent Press, London, 1955, 1957.
[2d ed.], Wm. B. Eerdmans, Grand Rapids, 1965.
[2d ed.], with an introduction by John E. Steely, Chanticleer
Publishing Co., Wake Forest, North Carolina, 1983.

2.12   *The Person and Place of Jesus Christ.* The Congregational Union
Lecture for 1909. London: Hodder & Stoughton. xix, 357 pp.

Microform editions:
Independent Press, London, 1978.
Pilgrim Press, Boston, 1989.
Reprintings:
Pilgrim Press, Boston, 1909, [1910], 1968.
[4th-6th impressions] Independent Press, London, 1909, 1910,
1930, 1946, 1948, 1951, 1955, 1961.
Eaton & Mains, New York, 1909.
[2nd-3d impressions] Hodder & Stoughton, London, 1910, 1911.
Jennings & Graham, Cincinnati, 1910.
Westminster Press, Philadelphia, 1910.
Wm. B. Eerdmans, Grand Rapids, 1961, 1964, 1965.

1910

2.13   *The Work of Christ.* The Expositor's Library. London-New York:
Hodder & Stoughton. xii, 244 pp.

Editions:
2d ed., with a Foreword by John S. Whale and a Memoir by
Jessie Forsyth Andrews, Independent Press, London, 1938.
xxxii, 244 pp. Includes list of author's books, xxix.

Microform editions:
[2d ed.], Independent Press, London, 1978.
[1st ed.], Hodder & Stoughton, London and New York, 1989.
Reprintings:
[1st ed.], Westminster Press, Toronto, 1910.
[1st ed.], Hodder & Stoughton, London, 1913.
[2d ed.], Independent Press, London, 1946, 1948, 1952, 1958.
[2d ed.], Collins: Fontana Library, London, 1965.

2.14   *The Power of Prayer.* With Dora Greenwell. Little Books on Religion. Edited by W. R. Nicoll. London: Hodder & Stoughton. v, 149 pp.

Forsyth's contributions, "Prayer as Incessant," pp. 55-92, and "Prayer as Insistent," pp. 95-149. Also published in *The Soul of Prayer* (1916), chapters 5 and 6.

Microform editions:
Hodder & Stoughton, London and New York, 1989.

1911

2.15   *Christ on Parnassus: Lectures on Art, Ethic, and Theology.* London-New York: Hodder & Stoughton. xii, 297 pp.

Microform editions:
Hodder & Stoughton, London and New York, 1990.
Reprintings:
Independent Press, London, 1911, 1959.
Allenson, London, 1959.

1912

2.16   *Faith, Freedom and the Future.* London-New York: Hodder & Stoughton. xvi, 348 pp.

Editions:
[2d ed.], Independent Press, London, 1955. With a "Foreword" by Jessie Forsyth Andrews. Also includes "Declaration of the Faith, Church Order, and Discipline of the Congregation, or Independent Dissenters, adopted at the annual meeting of the Congregational Union, May, 1833," pp. 349-355.
Microform editions:
[1st ed.], Hodder & Stoughton, London and New York, 1990.
Reprintings:
[1st ed.], T. and A. Constable at the Edinburgh University Press, Edinburgh, 1912.

2.17 *Marriage; Its Ethic and Religion.* London-New York: Hodder & Stoughton. viii, 152 pp.

Expands a lecture delivered in connection with the National Council of Public Morals.

Microform editions:
Research Publications, New Haven, 1977.
Hodder & Stoughton, London, 1977.

2.18 *The Principle of Authority in Relation to Certainty, Sanctity and Society. An Essay in the Philosophy of Experimental Religion.* London-New York: Hodder & Stoughton. x, 475 pp.

Often cited with a publication date of 1913, according to *The English Catalogue of Books* the volume was actually published in December 1912.

Editions:
2d ed., Independent Press, London, 1952. x, 430 pp.
Microform editions:
[1st ed.], Lost Cause Press, Louisville, 1976.
[1st ed.], Hodder & Stoughton, London and New York, 1990.

1915

2.19 *Theology in Church and State.* London-New York: Hodder & Stoughton. xxvi, 328 pp.

1916

2.20 *The Christian Ethic of War.* London: Longmans, Green, and Co. x, 196 pp.

2.21 *The Justification of God: Lectures for War-time on a Christian Theodicy.* Studies in Theology, 23. London: Duckworth. viii, 232 pp.

Often cited with a publication date of 1917, according to *The English Catalogue of Books* the volume was actually published in November 1916.

Editions:
[2d ed.], omitting author's preface and with a foreword by D. R. Davies, Latimer House, London, 1948. 224 pp.
Reprintings:
[1st ed.], C. Scribner's Sons, New York, 1917.
[1st ed.], Duckworth, London, 1917.
[2d ed.], Duckworth Press, London, 1948.
[2d ed.], Independent Press, London, [1948], 1957.

2.22   *The Soul of Prayer*. London: C. H. Kelly. 140 pp.

Includes Forsyth's contribution from *The Power of Prayer* (1910).

Editions:
   2d ed., Independent Press, London, [1949]. 92 pp.
Reprintings:
   [1st ed.], Wm. B. Eerdmans, Grand Rapids, 1916.
   [1st ed.], Epworth, London, [192?].
   [2d ed.], Independent Press, London, 1951, 1966 (5th impr.).
   [2d ed.], Wm B. Eerdmans, Grand Rapids, 1960, 1965.
   [2d ed.], Schmul Publishing Company, Salem, Ohio, 1986.

1917

2.23   *Lectures on the Church and the Sacraments*. London: Longmans, Green. xiv, 289 pp.

Editions:
   [2d ed.], *The Church and the Sacraments*, with H. T. Andrews; with a preface by J. K. Mozley and a note by Jessie Forsyth Andrews, Independent Press, London, [1947]. xxii, 309 pp.
   [3d ed.], Independent Press, London, 1949.
Reprintings:
   [1st ed.], Independent Press, London, 1917.
   [3d ed.], Independent Press, London, 1953, 1955, 1964.

1918

2.24   *This Life and the Next: The Effect on This Life of Faith in Another*. London-New York: Macmillan. vii, 127 pp.

Editions:
   [2d ed.], Independent Press, London, 1946. 87 pp.
Reprintings:
   [1st ed.], Pilgrim Press, Boston, 1948. 111 pp.
   [2d ed.], Independent Press, London, 1953.

3. Contributions to Books

1884

3.1   "A Tribute, a Reminiscence, and a Study." In *In Memoriam: James Baldwin Brown*, ed. by Elizabeth B. Brown, 133ff. London: James Clarke.

<u>1893</u>

3.2   "Revelation and the Person of Christ." In *Faith and Criticism: Essays by Congregationalists*, 2d ed., 95-144. London: Sampson Low, Marston and Co.; New York: E. P. Dutton.

<u>1900</u>

3.3   Article III. In *The Atonement in Modern Religious Thought: A Theological Symposium*, ed. by Frederic Godet, 59-88. London: James Clarke.

3.4   Essay. In *Different Conceptions of Priesthood and Sacrifice*, ed. by W. Sanday, 174ff. London: Longmans, Green.

3.5   "The Cross as the Final Seat of Authority." In *Proceedings of the Second International Congregational Council*. Boston: Usher.

<u>1903</u>

3.6   "The Problem of Forgiveness in the Lord's Prayer" and "Bring Us Not Into Temptation." In *The Sermon on the Mount*, v. 2: *A Practical Exposition of the Lord's Prayer (Matthew 6:9-13)*, 181-207. Manchester: James Robinson.

<u>1906</u>

3.7   "When We Were Boys." In *Bon Record. Records and Reminiscences of Aberdeen Grammar School*, ed. by H. F. Morland Simpson, 259-261. Aberdeen: D. Wylie and Son.

3.8   "A Holy Church the Moral Guide of Society" and "The Grace of the Gospel as the Moral Authority in the Church." In *Congregational Year Book*, 15-97. London: Congregational Union of England and Wales.

<u>1907</u>

3.9   "Church and University." In *Record of the Celebration of the Quartercentenary of the University of Aberdeen*, ed. by P. J. Anderson, 315-325. Aberdeen: University of Aberdeen.

3.10   "Immanence and Incarnation." In *The Old Faith and the New Theology*, ed. by Charles H. Vine, 47-61. London: Sampson Low, Marston and Co.

1908

3.11   "Introduction." In *The Inspiration and Authority of Holy Scripture*, by J. Monro Gibson, vii-xviii. Christian Faith and Doctrine Series, 1. London: Thomas Law.

Reprinted by Fleming H. Revell, New York, 1912.

3.12   "Forgiveness Through Atonement the Essential of Evangelical Christianity." In *Proceedings of the Third International Congregational Council*, ed. by J. Brown, 28-53. London: Congregational Union of England and Wales.

Also published in *British Congregationalist* (2 July 1908); in *The Cruciality of the Cross* (1909); and in *Revelation Old and New* (1962).

1909

3.13   "Pastoralia." In *The Cure of Souls*, ed. by Harry Escott, 107-136. Grand Rapids, Michigan: William B. Eerdmans, 1971.

Spiritual direction given to students in 1909.

1911

3.14   "Christ and the Christian Principle." In *London Theological Studies*, by members of the Faculty of Theology in the University of London, 133-166. London: University of London Press.

1918

3.15   "Reconstruction and Religion." In *Problems of Tomorrow*, ed. by F. A. Rees, 15-23. London: James Clarke.

1919

3.16   "Unity and Theology." In *Towards Reunion*, by Church of England and Free Church Writers, 51-81. London: Macmillan.

1920

3.17   Eulogy. In *The Life of Charles Silvester Horne*, by W. B. Selbie, 302ff. London: Hodder & Stoughton.

3.18   Preface. In *In the Shadow of an Agony*, by Oswald Chambers. 2d ed. London: n.p.

1922

3.19   Essay. In *John Hunter, D.D. A Life*, by Leslie S. Hunter, 2d ed., 289ff. London: Hodder & Stoughton.

4. Letters to the Editor

1877

4.1   "Religious Communism." *English Independent* (1 November): 1202-3.

4.2   Letter. *English Independent* (8 November): 1230ff.

1887

4.3   "Preachers and Politics." *The Manchester Examiner and Times* (29 December): 5.

On the Irish question and government policy, by "Publicola," Forsyth's pseudonym. Letters of reply were written by Morgan Brierly and "A Nonconformist Minister," *The Manchester Examiner and Times*, 31 December.

1892

4.4   Letter. *Congregational Monthly* 5 (January): 2.

1896

4.5   Letter. *British Weekly* 20 (24 September): 356.

1900

4.6   "Dr. Barrett and Higher Criticism." *Examiner* (30 August): 580; (20 September): 650-651.

1901

4.7   Letter. *Examiner* (1 August): 320.

1903

4.8   Letter. *Examiner* (12 November): 476.

1904

4.9   "Self-Sacrifice." *Examiner* (7 January): 5.

1905

4.10   "The Attacks on the Churches." *British Weekly* 37 (23 March): 614; (30 March): 638.

4.11   Letter. *British Weekly* 38 (18 May): 143.

4.12   "Our Colleges." *Examiner* (29 June): 620.

4.13   "Dr. Forsyth and Mysticism." *Examiner* (9 November): 434.

1906

4.14   Letter. *British Weekly* 40 (12 July): 344.

4.15   Letters on Chinese labor. *Times* (London) (18 January): 4; (20 January): 12; (25 January): 11; (26 January): 7; (29 January): 7.

1907

4.16   Letter. *British Weekly* 43 (31 October): 83.

1908

4.17   Letter. *Christian World* (26 March): 11.

4.18   Letter. *Christian World* (10 September): 3.

4.19   "Law and Atonement." *Christian World* (24 September): 9.

1910

4.20   Letter. *British Weekly* 48 (19 May): 172.
       Also appears in *British Congregationalist* (19 May): 418.

4.21   "Welfare and Charity." *British Congregationalist* (24 November): 439-440.

1911

4.22   Letter. *British Weekly* 51 (26 October): 100.

1913

4.23   "The Church and the Children." *British Weekly* 54 (15 May): 169.

1915

4.24   "Dr. Forsyth and Mr. Campbell." *British Weekly* 59 (4 November): 93.

4.25   "The Colleges and Recruiting." *British Weekly* 59 (18 November): 134.

Signed by Forsyth, Garvie, Selbie, and Bennett.

1916

4.26   "The Rev. R. J. Campbell." *British Weekly* 59 (6 January): 284.

1917

4.27   "The Village Churches and the War." *British Weekly* 61 (29 March): 496.

1919

4.28   "Church and Nation: A Nonconformist on the Enabling Bill." *Times* (London) (28 May): 8; (29 May): 8; (6 June): 8; (16 June): 8.

Regarding the Church of England National Assembly Bill.

4.29   "One Step to Reunion: Interchange of Pulpits." *Times* (London) (30 August): 6.

On the interchange of pulpits between the Church of England and the Free Churches. Signed by Forsyth, R. C. Gillie, J. H. Jowett, J. Scott Lidgett, W. B. Selbie, J. H. Shakespeare, and P. Carnegie Simpson.

5. Pamphlets

1878

5.1   *Maid, Arise!* Bradford: T. Brear. 19 pp.

5.2   *The Weariness of Modern Life.* n.p. 16 pp.

1884

5.3   *Baldwin Brown: A Tribute, a Reminiscence, and a Study.* London: James Clarke and Co. 20 pp.

1885

5.4   *The Pulpit and the Age.* Installation sermon at Cheetham Hill Congregational Church, Manchester. Manchester: Brook and Chrystal. 16 pp.

1886

5.5   *Socialism and Christianity in Some of Their Deeper Aspects.* Manchester: Brook and Chrystal. 37 pp.

1889

5.6   *The Antiquity of Dissent.* Manchester: Brook and Chrystal. 32 pp.

1891

5.7   *The Old Faith and the New.* Manchester: Brook and Chrystal. iv, 28 pp.

Also published as follows: Leicester: Midland Educational Company, 1891.

1896

5.8   *Intercessory Services for Aid in Public Worship.* Manchester: John Heywood. 29 pp.

1898

5.9   *The Happy Warrior: A Sermon on the Death of Mr. Gladstone, May 22, 1898.* London: H. R. Allenson. 30 pp.

1899

5.10   *Priesthood and Its Theological Assumptions.* Free Church Tracts for the Times, no. 3. London: National Council of Evangelical Free Churches, 1898-1899. 16 pp.

1902

5.11   *Holy Christian Empire.* London: James Clarke. 46 pp.

First published in the *Christian World Pulpit* (May 1902). Also appears in *Missions in State and Church* (1908), chapter 10.

1903

5.12   *The Courage of Faith.* Glasgow: Wm. Asher. 16 pp.

5.13   *The New Congregationalism and the New Testament Congregationalism.* Sydney: William Brooks and Co.

1905

5.14   *A Holy Church the Moral Guide of Society.* London: Congregational Union of England and Wales. 68 pp.

An address delivered in the City Temple. Also published in the *British Weekly* (11 May), the *Congregational Year Book* (1906), and in *The Church, the Gospel and Society* (1962).

5.15   *The Grace of the Gospel as the Moral Authority in the Church.* London: Congregational Union of England and Wales. 67 pp.

An address delivered in the Coliseum, Leeds, on Tuesday, October 10, 1905. Also appears in the *Congregational Year Book* (1906), and in *The Church, the Gospel and Society* (1962).

1909

5.16   *Monism.* London: Society for the Study of Religions. 16 pp.

1911

5.17   *Revelation Old and New*. Edinburgh: Blackwood. 16 pp.

Reprinted by Independent Press, London, 1962.

5.18   "The United States of the Church." In *A United Free Church of England*, 15-47. With J. H. Shakespeare. London: F. B. Meyer. 52 pp.

Also published in *The Church and the Sacraments*, chapter 6.

5.19   *The Story of the Scottish Congregational Theological Hall 1811-1911*, 20-22. Edinburgh: Morrison and Gibb.

1914

5.20   *A Radiant Life: In Memory of Charles Silvester Horne*. n.p. 8 pp.

1916

5.21   "Church, Ministry and Sacraments." In *The Validity of the Congregational Ministry*. With J. V. Bartlet and J. D. Jones. London: Congregational Union of England and Wales. 52 pp.

1917

5.22   *Reunion and Recognition*. London: Congregational Union of England and Wales, 1917. 24 pp.

Also published in *Congregationalism and Reunion, Two Lectures* (1952).

1918

5.23   *Congregationalism and Reunion*. London: Congregational Union of England and Wales. 24 pp.

Also published in *Congregationalism and Reunion, Two Lectures* (1952).

5.24   *The Roots of a World Commonwealth*. London-New York: Hodder & Stoughton. 19 pp.

Reprinted by George H. Doran, New York, 1918; 2d ed. by Independent Press, London, 1952; and microfilmed by Hodder & Stoughton, London and New York, 1990.

5.25   *A Few Hints About Reading the Bible*. New York: Association Press. 23 pp.

Reprinted from the *Biblical Review*, 1918-1919.

1943

5.26   *The Glorious Gospel: An Abridgement of a Sermon Preached for the London Missionary Society, May 1903*. London Missionary Society. Triple Jubilee Papers, no. 3. London: Livingstone Press, 1943. 16 pp.

An abridgement of "The Fatherhood of Death" in *Missions in State and Church* (1908).

1950

5.27   *Christian Aspects of Evolution*. London: Epworth Press. 39 pp.

Reprinted from the *London Quarterly Review* (October 1905).

No Date

5.28   *Coleridge's "Ancient Mariner." An Exposition and Sermon from a Modern Text*. Bradford: Wm. Boyles and Sons. 19 pp.

5.29   *The Minister's Prayer*. London: National Council of Evangelical Free Churches.

5.30   *The Obligations of Doctrinal Subscription*.

In New College Library. Also published in *Modern Review* 2, no. 5 (1881): 273-281.

5.31   *Pfleiderer's View of St. Paul's Doctrine*. London: W. Speaght. 16 pp.

Also published in *Modern Review* 4 (1883): 81-86.

6. Periodical Articles

1878

6.1   "The Strength of Weakness." *Christian World Pulpit* 13 (6 February): 85-87.

1881

6.2   "The Obligations of Doctrinal Subscription." *Modern Review* 2, no. 5 (April): 252-281.

Also published as a pamphlet, n.d. Bound with other pamphlets in New College Library.

1882

6.3   "Egypt: A Sermon for Young Men." *Christian World Pulpit* 22 (1 November): 275-278.

1883

6.4   "Pfleiderer's View of St. Paul's Doctrine." *Modern Review* 4 (January): 81-96.

This review of Otto Pfleiderer's theology was also published as an undated pamphlet.

1884

6.5   "Pessimism." *Christian World Pulpit* 25 (16 January): 42-44.

1885

6.6   "The Argument for Immortality Drawn from the Nature of Love." *Christian World Pulpit* 28 (2 December): 360-364.

1887

6.7   "Sunday-Schools and Modern Theology." *Christian World Pulpit* 31 (23 February): 123-127.

1888

6.8   "The New Year." *Congregational Monthly* 1 (January): 13.

6.9   "The Relation of the Church to the Poor." *Congregational Monthly* 3 (March): n.p.

1889

6.10   "A Tribute" to Dr. Charles Berry. *British Weekly* (2 February): 310.

6.11   "Preaching and Poetry." *Expository Times* 1 (September): 269-272.

1891

6.12   "Teachers of the Century: Robert Browning." *The Modern Church* (15 October): 451-452.

6.13   "About Giving." *Examiner* (26 December): 756.

1892

6.14   "Faith and Charity." *Congregational Monthly* 5 (January): 13.

1893

6.15   "Words for the Times." *Congregational Monthly* 6 (July): 167.

1894

6.16   "A Pocket of Gold." *Independent and Nonconformist* (8 March): 187.

6.17   "Mystics and Saints." *Expository Times* 5 (June): 401-404.

1895

6.18   "Dr. Dale." *Sunday Magazine* 24 (May): 331-337.

6.19   "The Divine Self-Emptying." *Christian World Pulpit* 47 (1 May): 276-280.
Also published in *The Taste of Death and the Life of Grace*, 89-127.

1896

6.20   "The Holy Father." *Christian World Pulpit* 50 (7 October): 225-229.
Also published in *British Weekly* 21 (19 November): 74; (26 November): 94-95; *The Holy Father and the Living Christ* (1897); and reprinted in *Christian World Pulpit* 100 (30 November 1921): 254-259.

1897

6.21   "The Way of Life." *Wesleyan Methodist Magazine* 120 (n.d.): 83-88.

6.22   "God as Holy Father." *Homiletic Review* 33 (March): 234-236.
Reprinted from the *Christian World Pulpit* (1896).

6.23   "Theology in the Future." *Independent and Nonconformist* (10 June): n.p.

6.24   "The Living Christ." *British Weekly* 22 (22 July): 228-229.
Also published in *The Holy Father and the Living Christ* (1897) and *God the Holy Father* (1957).

6.25   "The Conversion of Faith by Love." *British Weekly* 23 (28 October): 22.
Revised and published in *Christ on Parnassus* (1911).

1898

6.26   "Sacramentalism the True Remedy for Sacerdotalism." *Expositor* 5th ser., 8 (September): 245-257; (October): 298-311.

1899

6.27   "A Hymn to Christ." *British Weekly* 26 (1 June): 133.
Poem.

6.28   "The Atonement in Modern Religious Thought: Persistence of the Doctrine." *The Christian World* (9 November): 11.

6.29   "The Cross as the Final Seat of Authority." *Contemporary Review* 76 (October): 589-609.
Also published in *Living Age* 7th ser., 223 (16 December): 671-687; in *Proceedings of the Second International Congregational Council* (1900); and in *The Gospel and Authority: A P. T. Forsyth Reader* (1971).

6.30   "Dr. Dale." *London Quarterly Review* 91 (April): 193-222.

1900

6.31   "The Slowness of God." *Expository Times* 11 (February): 218-222.

6.32   "Prayer." *British Weekly* 27 (22 February): 424.

6.33   "Does the Third Beatitude Fit the Englishman?" and "The Moral Peril of the Frontier Life." *Congregational Monthly*, n.s. 1 (April): 11.

6.34   "Dr. Martineau." *London Quarterly Review* 93 (April): 214-250.

6.35   "The Empire for Christ." *Christian World Pulpit* 57 (16 May): 303-311.

6.36   "Farewell Counsels to Students." *British Weekly* 28 (14 June): 179-180.

6.37   "Things New and Old in Heresy." *Examiner* (12 July): 399.

6.38   "A Simple Gospel." *British Weekly* 28 (11 October): 504

6.39   "The Taste of Death and the Life of Grace." *Christian World Pulpit* 58 (28 November): 296-302.

        Also published in the book of the same title (1901) and in *God the Holy Father* (1957).

6.40   "The Supreme Evidence of God's Love." *Examiner* (20 December): 167.

        1901

6.41   "The Power of the Resurrection." *Examiner* (11 April): 26.
        Also published in *Revelation Old and New* (1962).

6.42   "Dr. G. A. Smith's Yale Lecture." *British Weekly* 30 (25 April): 51-53.

6.43   "The Significance of the Church Fabric." *Christian World Pulpit* 59 (26 June): 415-418.

6.44   "The Courage of Faith." *Examiner* (11 July): 270-271.

6.45   "Treating the Bible Like Any Other Book." *British Weekly* 30 (15 August): 401-402.

6.46   "Notes from Pisgah." *British Weekly* 30 (3 October): 551.

6.47   "How to Read the Bible." *Examiner* (21 November): 647.

        1902

6.48   "Preachers and Politics." *Examiner* (6 February): 107; (13 February): 129.

6.49   "The Evangelical Experience." *Examiner* (17 April): 320-321.

6.50   "The Evangelical Basis of Free Churchism." *Contemporary Review* 81 (May): 680-695.

6.51   "Missions as the True Imperial and Apostolic Succession." *The Methodist Recorder* (8 May): 14-16.

Published as a pamphlet, *Holy Christian Empire* (1902); as "An Allegory of the Resurrection," *Christian World Pulpit* 61 (14 May): 312-319; and in *Missions in State and Church* (1908), chapter 10.

6.52   "The Depletion from the Ministry." *Examiner* (19 June): 555-556; (26 June): 586-587.

6.53   "Judgment." *Christian World Pulpit* 62 (1 October): 209.

Also published as "Judgment unto Salvation," *Examiner* (2 October): 332-335; and in *Missions in State and Church* (1908), chapter 2.

1903

6.54   "The Need for a Revival of Personal Religion." *Examiner* (26 March): 291-292.

Also revised and published in *Positive Preaching and the Modern Mind* (1907), chapter 5.

6.55   "The Charter of Missions." *Christian World Pulpit* 63 (20 May): 305-312.

Also published as a pamphlet: *The Glorious Gospel* (1943); and in *Missions in State and Church* (1908), chapter 3.

6.56   "The New Congregationalism and the New Testament Congregationalism." *Examiner* (4 June): 551-552; (11 June): 575-576.

6.57   "The Church, the State, the Priest, and the Future." *Examiner* (9 July): 27ff.; (16 July): 55ff.

6.58   "The Spiritual Reason for Passive Resistance." *Examiner* 2 (8 October): 2.

6.59   "Our Need of a Positive Gospel." *Examiner* (5 November): 462-463; (12 November): 486-487.

6.60   "The Christmas Miracle." *British Weekly* (23 December): 320.

1904

6.61   "The Need for a Positive Gospel." *London Quarterly Review* 101 (January): 64-99.

6.62   "The Paradox of Christ." *London Quarterly Review* 102 (June): 111-138.

6.63   "The Scotch Church Case: How It Strikes a Contemporary." *Examiner* (18 August): 144-145.

1905

6.64   "A New Year Message to the Churches." *Examiner* (5 January): 7-8.

6.65   "The Sects and the Public." *Examiner* (23 March): 262.

6.66   "A Holy Church the Moral Guide of Society." *British Weekly* 38 (11 May): 129.

Also published in the *Examiner* (11 May): 441-449; as a pamphlet (1905); in *The Congregational Year Book* (1906); and in *The Church, the Gospel and Society* (1962).

6.67   "Message from Principal Forsyth, D.D." *Congregational Monthly*, n.s. 6 (July): 74.

6.68   "Authority and Theology." *Hibbert Journal* 4 (October): 63-78.

Also published in *Living Age* 248 (6 January 1906): 18-27; and in *The Gospel and Authority: A P. T. Forsyth Reader* (1971).

6.69   "The Evangelical Churches and the Higher Criticism." *Contemporary Review* 88 (October): 574-599.

Also published in *The Gospel and Authority: A P. T. Forsyth Reader* (1971).

6.70   "Some Christian Aspects of Evolution." *London Quarterly Review* 104 (October): 209-239.

Also published in *Living Age* 247 (11 November): 323-341; and as a pamphlet by Epworth Press, London, 1950.

6.71   "The Grace of the Gospel as the Moral Authority in the Church." *Examiner* (12 October): 319-325.

6.72   "Appeal to the Archbishop of Canterbury." *Examiner* (19 October): 358-359.

6.73   "Appeal to the Primate." *Christian World* (19 October): 21-22.

6.74   "Federate on the Gospel of Grace." *Christian World* (30 November): 21.

Also published in "A Rallying Ground for the Free Churches" (1906).

6.75   "Preaching Christ and Preaching for Christ." *Examiner* (21 December): 574.

Also printed in *British Missionary* (January 1906).

1906

6.76   "The Chairman's Mantle." *Examiner* (11 January): 28.

Poem.

6.77   "The Place of Spiritual Experience in the Making of Theology." *Christian World* (15 March): 12.

Also expanded in *Christian World Pulpit* 69 (21 March): 184-187; and published in *Revelation Old and New* (1962).

6.78   "The Catholic Threat of Passive Resistance." *Contemporary Review* 89 (April): 562-567.

6.79   "A Rallying Ground for the Free Churches–The Reality of Grace." *Hibbert Journal* 4 (July): 824-844.

Also published in *The Gospel and Authority: A P. T. Forsyth Reader* (1971).

6.80   "Church and University." *British Congregationalist* (27 September): 201-202.

Also appears in the *Quartercentenary* of Aberdeen University (1907).

6.81   "The Church's One Foundation." *London Quarterly Review* 106 (October): 193-202.

Also published in *Living Age* 251 (10 November): 351-356; and in *The Gospel and Authority: A P. T. Forsyth Reader* (1971).

6.82   "The Ideal Ministry." *British Congregationalist* (18 October): 283-285.

Also published as "The Ideal Ministry of the Church," *Christian World* (18 October): 22; and in *Revelation Old and New* (1962).

6.83   "Virgin Birth." *British Congregationalist* (25 October): 318-319.

6.84   "Dr. Forsyth on the Education Crisis." *British Congregationalist* (8 November): 369.

6.85   "Church, State, Dogma and Education." *Contemporary Review* 90 (December): 827-836.

1907

6.86   "The New Theology: Immanence and Incarnation." *British Congregationalist* (24 January): 77-78.

Also published in *The Old Faith and the New Theology* (1907).

6.87   "The Newest Theology." *British Weekly* 41 (7 March): 581-582.

6.88   "The Apostolate of Negation." *British Congregationalist* (21 March): 271.

6.89   "The New Theology." *British Weekly* 41 (21 March): 637-638.

6.90   "God, Sin, and the Atonement." *British Weekly* 41 (28 March): 669-670.

6.91   "The Pastoral Duty of the Preacher." *British Congregationalist* (28 March): 247-248.

Also revised for *Positive Preaching and the Modern Mind* (1907), chapter 3.

6.92   "Dr. Forsyth on the Authority of Grace." *Primitive Methodist Quarterly Review* n.s., 29 (April) : 286-300.

6.93   "Address from the Chair." *British Congregationalist* (16 May): 489.

6.94   "The Minister's Prayer." *British Congregationalist* (6 June): 561.

Also published in The Power of Prayer (1910); in *The Soul of Prayer* (1916), chapter 6; as a separate pamphlet (n.d.); and in *Revelation Old and New* (1962).

6.95   "Sentiment and Sentimentalism." *British Congregationalist* (11 July): 22-23.

6.96   "Some Aspects of Spiritual Religion." *British Congregationalist* (15 August): 134.

6.97   "Motherhood." *British Congregationalist* (26 September): 255-256.

6.98   "National Purity Crusade." *British Congregationalist* (3 October): 273.

6.99   "The Union and the Railway Dispute." *British Congregationalist* (24 October): 361.

6.100   "Sociality, Socialism, and the Church." *British Congregationalist* (28 November): 487-488; (5 December): 509-510; (12 December): 534-535; (19 December): 561-562.

Also published in *Socialism, the Church and the Poor* (1908), part I.

6.101   *Alma Mater*. Aberdeen University (18 December): 110ff.

1908

6.102   "The Love of Liberty and the Love of Truth." *Contemporary Review* 93 (February): 158-170.

Also published in *Living Age* 256 (28 March): 771-780.

6.103   "To the Congregational Churches of England and Wales." *British Weekly* 43 (27 February): 556.

An open letter from the former chairmen and the college principals.

6.104   "Christ at the Gate." *Christian World Pulpit* 73 (18 March): 177-182.

6.105   "The Distinctive Thing in Christian Experience." *Hibbert Journal* 6 (April): 481-499.

Also published in *The Person and Place of Jesus Christ* (1909), chapter 7; and in *The Gospel and Authority: A P. T. Forsyth Reader* (1971).

6.106   "The Faith of Congregationalism." With A. E. Garvie. *British Congregationalist* (18 June): 593.

6.107   "Prayer and Its Importunity." *London Quarterly Review* 110 (July): 1-22.

Also published in *The Soul of Prayer* (1916), chapter 6; and in *The Power of Prayer* (1910).

6.108   "Forgiveness through Atonement the Essential of Evangelical Christianity." *British Congregationalist* (2 July): 2.

Also published in the *Proceedings of the Third International Congregational Council* (1908), and revised in *The Cruciality of the Cross* (1909).

6.109   "What is Meant by the Blood of Christ?" *Expositor* 7th ser., 6 (September): 207-225.

Published in *The Cruciality of the Cross* (1909), chapter 4.

6.110 "What is the Evangelical Faith?" *British Congregationalist* (10 September): 217-218; (17 September): 239-240; (24 September): 257-258.

6.111 "Some Christmas Thoughts." *British Congregationalist* (24 December): 553.

1909

6.112 "The Churches and Bible Study." *Christian World* (18 February): 5.

6.113 "Miraculous Healing, Then and Now." *British Congregationalist* (11 March): 194.

6.114 "The Insufficiency of Social Righteousness as a Moral Ideal." *Hibbert Journal* 7 (April): 596-613.

Also published in *Living Age* 261 (26 June): 779-789; and in *The Cruciality of the Cross* (1909), chapter 3.

6.115 "Lay Religion." *British Congregationalist* (29 April): 337-338; (6 May): 357-358.

Also published in *The Person and Place of Jesus Christ* (1909), chapter 1; and in *Revelation Old and New* (1962).

6.116 "The Person and Place of Jesus Christ." *British Congregationalist* (6 May): 356; (13 May); 375; (20 May): 407; (27 May): 440; (3 June): 467; (10 June): 480; (17 June): 500; (24 June): 520.

Also published as a book under the same title (1909).

6.117 "Theological Reaction." *British Weekly* 46 (13 May): 150.

6.118 "An Open Letter to a Young Minister on Certain Questions of the Hour." *The Christian World* (27 May): 11; (3 June): 14.

6.119 "The Evidential Value of Miracles." *London Quarterly Review* 112 (July): 1-7.

6.120 "The Roman Road of Rationalism: What do the Advanced Critics Ask Us to Give Up?" *The Christian World* 60 (26 August): 6; (2 September): 3.

6.121 "The Faith of Jesus." *Expository Times* 21 (October): 8-9.

Comment on Adolf Schlatter's *New Testament Theology*.

6.122   "Modernism: Home and Foreign."   *British Congregationalist* (14 October): 303, 323-326.

Also published in the *Christian World* (14 October): 22-23.

6.123   "The Peers or the People." *Christian World* (16 December): 4.

6.124   "The Interest and Duty of Congregationalists in the Present Crisis: A Symposium." *British Congregationalist* (23 December): 539.

6.125   "The Modern Ministry: Its Duties and Perils. Interview With Dr. Forsyth." *British Congregationalist* (30 December): 559.

6.126   "Orthodoxy, Heterodoxy, Heresy, and Freedom." *Hibbert Journal* 8 (December 1909/January 1910): 321-329.

1910

6.127   "Messages from the Progressive Leaders." *British Weekly* 47 (6 January): 421.

6.128   "The Word and the World." *British Weekly* 47 (10 February): [533]-534.

6.129   "Theological Liberalism v. Liberal Theology." *British Weekly* 47 (17 February): 557-558.

6.130   "The Attitude of the Church to the Present Unrest." *British Congregationalist* (17 March): 214-215.

6.131   "God Takes a Text and Preaches." *British Weekly* 48 (14 April): 36.

6.132   "Missions the Soul of Civilization." *Christian World Pulpit* 77 (4 May): 273-277.

6.133   "Calvinism and Capitalism." *Contemporary Review* 97 (June): 728-741; 98 (July): 74-87.

6.134   "Intellectual Difficulties to Faith." *The Record* (22 July): 708-710.

1911

6.135   "Is Anything Wrong With Our Churches? A Symposium." *British Congregationalist* (19 January): 46.

6.136   "The Majesty and Mercy of God." *British Congregationalist* (4 May): 367.

Also published in *Revelation Old and New* (1962).

6.137   "Majesty and Mercy." *Christian World Pulpit* 79 (17 May): 305-307.

6.138   "Church Statistics." *British Weekly* (15 June): 284.

6.139   "Plebiscite and Gospel." *Contemporary Review* 100 (July): 60-76.

Also published in *The Principle of Authority* (1912), chapter 13.

6.140   "The Duty of the Christian Ministry." *British Congregationalist* (13 July): 27.

6.141   "The Goodness of God." *British Congregationalist* (10 August): 97.

Also published in *Revelation Old and New* (1962)

6.142   "Revelation and the Bible." *Hibbert Journal* 10 (October): 235-252.

Also published in *The Gospel and Authority: A P. T. Forsyth Reader* (1971).

6.143   "The Soul of Christ and the Cross of Christ." *London Quarterly Review* 116 (October): 193-212.

Also published in *The Gospel and Authority: A P. T. Forsyth Reader* (1971).

6.144   "Marriage: Its Ethic and Religion." *British Congregationalist* (30 November): 403.

Also expanded and published as a book under the same title (1912).

1912

6.145   "New Year Messages: How Congregationalists Should Meet 1912." *British Congregationalist* (4 January): 3.

6.146   "The Doctrinal Method." *British Congregationalist* (15 February): 114.

6.147   "Tribute to Dr. Fairbairn." *British Congregationalist* (15 February): 116.

Reprinted from the *Westminster Gazette*, 12 February.

6.148   "Tribute to Principal Fairbairn." *British Weekly* 51 (15 February): 568, 574.

6.149   "Liberty and Its Limits in the Church." *Contemporary Review* 101 (April): 502-512.

   Also published in *The Principle of Authority* (1912), chapter 14.

6.150   "The Home Rule Bill." *British Congregationalist* (18 April): 259.

6.151   "Self-Denial and Self-Committal." *Expositor*, 8th ser., 4 (July): 32-43.

6.152   "Faith and Mind." *Methodist Quarterly Review* 61 (October): 627-643.

6.153   "The Divorce Commission Report. Opinions of Prominent Congregationalists." *British Congregationalist* (21 November): 847.

6.154   "Intellectualism and Faith." *Hibbert Journal* 11 (December 1912/ January 1913): 311-328.

   1913

6.155   "The Religious Strength of Theological Reserve." *British Weekly* 53 (13 February): [577]-578.

6.156   "The Fund and the Faith." *British Weekly* 54 (29 May): 219.

6.157   "Congregationalism and the Principle of Liberty." *Constructive Quarterly* 1 (September): 498-521.

6.158   "The Church and Society." *Westminster Gazette* (6 September): 3; (13 September): 13; (20 September): 2.

6.159   "Land Laws of the Bible." *Contemporary Review* 104 (October): 496-504.

6.160   "The Church and Society–Alien or Allied?" *British Weekly* 55 (9 October): 43.

6.161   "Things New and Old." *Christian World Pulpit* 84 (29 October): 273-276.

6.162   "The Church and Divorce." *British Congregationalist* (30 October): 885.

   1914

6.163   "Christianity and Society." *Methodist Quarterly Review* 63, no. 1 (January): 3-21.

   Also published in the *British Weekly* (9 October 1913): 43.

6.164   "The Man and the Message." *London Quarterly Review* 121 (January): 1-11.

6.165   "Music and Worship." *Homiletic Review* 67 (January): 18-22.

Also published in the *Congregational Quarterly* 33 (October 1955): 339-344.

6.166   "Wedded Churches." *Daily Chronicle* (21 February): n.p.

Reviewed in the *British Congregationalist* (26 February 1914): 156.

6.167   "The Effectiveness of the Ministry." *British Congregationalist* (12 March): 198-199.

Also published in the *London Quarterly Review* 122 (July): 1-20; and in *The Church and the Sacraments* (1917), chapter 7.

6.168   "The Late Rev. C. S. Horne–A Tribute." *British Weekly* 56 (7 May): 140.

6.169   "The Church and the Nation." *Westminster Gazette* (12 May): 1ff.

Also published in the *British Congregationalist* (14 May): 383.

6.170   "Funeral Address for Silvester Horne." *British Congregationalist* (21 May): 421-422.

6.171   "Progress of the Free Churches: Religion and the State." *Times* (London) (25 May): 30.

By "A Nonconformist Correspondent."

6.172   "Our Experience of a Triune God." *Cambridge Christian Life* 1 (June): 240-246.

6.173   "The Church and the Nation–In Education, For Instance." *Westminster Gazette* (6 July): 1-2.

6.174   "Principal Forsyth on 'Church and State.'" *British Congregationalist* (9 July): 40.

Extracts from an article in the *Westminster Gazette* (6 July).

6.175   "Christianity and Nationality." *British Weekly* 56 (9 July): 385-386.

6.176   "Regeneration, Creation, and Miracle." *Methodist Quarterly Review* 63 (October): 627-643; 64 (January 1915): 89-103.

1915

6.177   "Dr. Forsyth on Evangelical Experience." *Methodist Review* 97 (January): 118-132.

6.178   "For the Fraternal." *Christian World* (14 February): n.p.

6.179   "The Conquest of Time by Eternity." *Christian World Pulpit* 87 (17 February): 104-108.

Also published in *The Justification of God* (1916), chapter 12.

6.180   "The Preaching of Jesus and the Gospel of Christ." *Expositor*, 8th ser. 9 (April): 325-335, (May): 404-421; 8th ser. 10 (July): 66-89, (August): 117-138, (October): 340-364, (November): 445-465.

6.181   "Veracity, Reality, and Regeneration." *London Quarterly Review* 123 (April): 193-216.

6.182   "Churches, Sects, and Wars." *Contemporary Review* 107 (May): 618-626.

6.183   "Faith, Metaphysic, and Incarnation." *Methodist Review* 97 (September): 696-719.

6.184   "History and Judgment." *Contemporary Review* 108 (October): 457-470.

Also published in *The Justification of God* (1916), chapter 11.

6.185   "Ibsen's Treatment of Guilt." *Hibbert Journal* 14 (October): 105-122.

6.186   "Prayer." *London Quarterly Review* 124 (October): 214-231.

Also published in *The Soul of Prayer* (1916), chapter 1.

6.187   "Lay Religion." *Constructive Quarterly* 3 (December): 767-789.

1916

6.188   "The First and Second Adam." *Methodist Review* 98 (May): 347-351.

6.189   "The Spiritual Needs in the Churches." *Christian World Pulpit* 89 (3 May): 251-255.

6.190   "The Conversion of the 'Good?'" *Contemporary Review* 109 (June): 760-771.

6.191 "Christ–King or Genius?" *Methodist Quarterly Review* 65, no. 3 (July): 433-447.

6.192 "Mr. Campbell's Book." *Christian World* (2 November): n.p.

6.193 "The Truncated Mind." *Manchester Guardian Weekly* (4 November): 5.

1917

6.194 "Christ's Person and His Cross." *Methodist Quarterly Review* 66, no. 1 (January): 3-22.

6.195 "The Cross of Christ as the Moral Principle of Society." *Methodist Review* 99 (January): 9-21.

6.196 "The Preacher and the Publicist." *London Quarterly Review* 127 (January): 1-18.

6.197 "The Efficiency and Sufficiency of the Bible." *Biblical Review* 2 (January): 10-30.

6.198 "The Need of a Church Theory for Church Unity." *Contemporary Review* 111 (March): 357-365.

Also enlarged for *The Church and the Sacraments* (1917), chapter 3.

6.199 "The Future of the Ministry." *The Christian World* (23 August): 4.

6.200 "The Moralization of Religion." *London Quarterly Review* 128 (October): 161-174.

6.201 "Comments on a Paper at the Congregational Union." *British Congregationalist* (19 October): 297-298.

6.202 "The Conditions of Evangelicalism." *Christian World* (13 December): n.p.

1918

6.203 "Some Effects of War on Belief." *Holborn Record* (January): 16-26.

6.204 "The Unborn, the Once Born, and the First Born." *The Christian World* (14 February): n.p.

6.205 "The Unity Beneath Reunion." *The Challenge* (15 February): n.p.

6.206 "Testamentary Ethics." *London Quarterly Review* 129 (April): 169-179.

6.207   "The Reality of God: A War-time Question." *Hibbert Journal* 16 (July): 608-619.

6.208   "Evangelicals and Home Reunion." *The Churchman* 32 (September): 528-536.

6.209   "A Few Hints About Reading the Bible." *Biblical Review* 3 (October): 530-544.

1919

6.210   "The Foolishness of Preaching." *Expository Times* 30 (January): 153-154.

6.211   "Religion, Private and Public." *London Quarterly Review* 131 (January): 19-32.

6.212   "The Inner Life of Christ." *Constructive Quarterly* 7 (March): 149-162.

6.213   "Religion and Reality." *Contemporary Review* 115 (May): 548-554.

1920

6.214   "Does the Church Prolong the Incarnation?" *London Quarterly and Holborn Review* 133 (January): 1-12; (April): 204-212.

1923

6.215   "The Preaching of Jesus and the Gospel of Christ." *Expositor* 25 (January-June): 288-312.

Continues the series published in 1915.

1943

6.216   "The Authority of the Cross: A Paper of 1906 by Dr. Robert Mackintosh, with Annotations by Dr. P. T. Forsyth." *Congregational Quarterly* 21 (July 1943): 209-218.

1950

6.217   "How to Help Your Minister." *The Christian World* (24 August 1950).

Also published in *Revelation Old and New* (1962).

1955

6.218 "Music and Worship." *Congregational Quarterly* 33 (October): 339-344.

Reprinted from the *Homiletic Review* (January 1914).

7. Reviews of Books and Articles

1883

7.1 "Auguste Bouvier, 'Le divin d'après les apôtres'" et "Paroles de foi et de liberté." ["The Divine according to the Apostles" and "Words of Faith and Freedom"] With Minna Forsyth. *Modern Review* 4: 410-413.

1884

7.2 "Nouvelles paroles de foi et de liberté." [New Words of Faith and Freedom] *Modern Review* 5: 379-381.

1900

7.3 "A Study of Dr. Martineau." *Examiner* (6 December): 129.

1901

7.4 "Mackintosh's *A Primer of Apologetics.*" *Examiner* (10 January): 222.

1903

7.5 "Sanctity and Certainty." *Examiner* (23 July): 86.

1909

7.6 "Nonconformity and Politics." *British Congregationalist* (4 February): 85-86.

7.7 "Milton's God and Milton's Satan." *Contemporary Review* 95 (April): 450-465.

Also published in *Living Age* 261 (29 May): 519-530.

7.8   "Sir Joseph Compton Rickett's New Book." *British Weekly* 46 (13 May): 122.

7.9   "Authority in Religion." *British Congregationalist* (23 December): 538.

1912

7.10   "The Pessimism of Mr. Thomas Hardy." *London Quarterly Review* 118 (October): 193-219.

Also published in *Living Age* 275 (23 November): 458-473.

7.11   "Mackintosh on the Person of Christ." *British Weekly* (28 November): 281-282.

LITERATURE ABOUT
P. T. FORSYTH

8. Books

8.1   Bradley, William L. *P. T. Forsyth: The Man and His Work*. London: Independent Press, 1952. 284 pp.

Based on dissertation.

8.2   Brown, Robert M. *P. T. Forsyth, Prophet for Today*. Philadelphia: Westminster Press, 1952. 191 pp.

Based on dissertation.

8.3   Griffith, Gwilym O. *The Theology of P. T. Forsyth*. London: Lutterworth Press, 1948. 104 pp.

8.4   Hunter, A. M. *P. T. Forsyth: Per Crucem ad Lucem*. London: SCM Press, 1974. 124 pp.

8.5   Miller, Donald G., Browne Barr, and Robert S. Paul. *P. T. Forsyth– The Man, the Preacher's Theologian, Prophet for the 20th Century: A Contemporary Assessment*. The Pittsburgh Theological Monograph Series, 36. Pittsburgh: Pickwick Press, 1981. xiii, 374 pp.

Contains a reprint of *Positive Preaching and Modern Mind*.

8.6   Pitt, Clifford S. *Church, Ministry and Sacraments: A Critical Evaluation of the Thought of Peter Taylor Forsyth*. Washington, D.C.: University Press of America, 1983. xxxii, 328 pp.

Based on dissertation.

8.7   Rodgers, J. H. *The Theology of P. T. Forsyth: The Cross of Christ and the Revelation of God*. London: Independent Press, 1965. xii, 324 pp.

9. Encyclopedia and Dictionary Articles

9.1   Brauer, Jerald C., ed. *The Westminster Dictionary of Church History*. Philadelphia: Westminster Press, 1971. S.v. "Forsyth, Peter Taylor," 333-334.

9.2   Campenhausen, Hans. Frhr. V., et al., eds. *Die Relgion in Geschichte und Gegenwart: Handwörterbuch für Theologie und Religionswissenschaft*, 3 Auflage. Tübingen: J. C. B. Mohr, 1986. S.v. "Forsyth, Peter Taylor," by H.-H. Schrey, Bd. 2, 1006.

9.3   Cross, F. L. and E. A. Livingstone, eds. *The Oxford Dictionary of the Christian Church*. 2d ed. London: Oxford University Press, 1974. S.v. "Forsyth, Peter Taylor," 524.

9.4   Douglas, J. D., Walter A. Elwell, and Peter Toon, eds. *The Concise Dictionary of the Christian Tradition*. Grand Rapids: Zondervan, 1989. S.v. "Forsyth, Peter Taylor," 156.

9.5   Douglas, J. D., gen. ed. *The New International Dictionary of the Christian Church*. Exeter: Paternoster Press, 1974. S.v. "Forsyth, Peter Taylor," by Haddon Willmer, 382-383.

9.6   ———, ed. *New Twentieth-Century Encyclopedia of Religious Knowledge*. 2d ed. Grand Rapids: Baker Book House, 1991. S.v. "Forsyth, Peter Taylor," by Raymond W. Albright, 336.

9.7   Elwell, Walter A., ed. *Evangelical Dictionary of Theology*. Grand Rapids: Baker Book House, 1984. S.v. "Forsyth, Peter Taylor," by Donald G. Bloesch, 422-423.

9.8   *Encyclopaedia Britannica*, 11th ed. (1910). S.v. "Forsyth, Peter Taylor," 10:677; 13th ed. (1926), 2:74.

9.9   Gentz, William H., ed. *The Dictionary of Bible and Religion*. Nashville: Abingdon Press, 1986. S.v. "Forsyth, Peter Taylor," 368.

9.10 Hastings, James, ed. *Encyclopedia of Religion and Ethics*. Edinburgh: T. & T. Clark, 1927.

      Cites Forsyth's views on Atonement, 9:722; Christology, 7:546; Conversion, 4:109; and Holiness, 6:745, 749.

9.11 Hughes, Philip E., ed. *The Encyclopedia of Christianity*. Marshallton, Delaware: The National Foundation for Christian Education, 1972. S.v. "Forsyth, Peter Taylor," by John H. Rodgers, 4:233-234.

9.12 Jackson, Samuel Macauley, et al., eds. *The New Schaff-Herzog Encyclopedia of Religious Knowledge*. New York and London: Funk and Wagnalls Company, 1909. S.v. "Forsyth, Peter Taylor," 4:345.

9.13 Loetscher, Lefferts A., ed. *Twentieth Century Encyclopedia of Religious Knowledge*. An Extension of The New Schaff-Herzog Encyclopedia of Religious Knowledge. Grand Rapids: Baker Book House, 1955. S.v. "Forsyth, Peter Taylor," by Raymond W. Albright, 1:438.

9.14 McKim, Donald K., ed. *Encyclopedia of the Reformed Faith*. Louisville: Westminster/John Knox Press, 1992. S.v. "Forsyth, Peter Taylor," by Donald G. Miller, 142.

9.15 Meagher, Paul K., Thomas C. O'Brien and Consuelo Maria Aherne, eds. *Encyclopedic Dictionary of Religion*. Washington, D.C.: Corpus Publications, 1979. S.v. "Forsyth, Peter Taylor," 2:1381.

9.16 *New Catholic Encyclopedia*, 1967 ed. S.v. "Forsyth, Peter Taylor," by W. Hannah, 5:1029-1030.

9.17 *The New Encyclopaedia Britannica*, 15th ed., (1989). S.v. "Forsyth, Peter Taylor," 4:889.

9.18 O'Brien, T. C., ed. *Corpus Dictionary of Western Churches*. Washington, D.C.: Corpus Publications, 1970. S.v. "Forsyth, Peter Taylor," 330.

9.19 *Who Was Who 1916-1928*, 1947 ed. S.v. "Forsyth, Rev. Dr. Peter Taylor," 369-370.

10. Essays, Articles or Parts in Books

10.1 Anderson, Marvin W. "Introduction." In *The Gospel and Authority: A P. T. Forsyth Reader*, 11-14. Minneapolis: Augsburg, 1971.

10.2 Andrews, Jessie Forsyth. "Memoir." In *The Work of Christ*, 2d ed., by P. T. Forsyth, vii-xxviii. London: Independent Press, 1938.

10.3 Barr, Browne. "P. T. Forsyth: The Preachers' Theologian–A Witness and Confession." In *P. T. Forsyth; The Man, the Preachers' Theologian, Prophet for the 20th Century: A Contemporary Assessment*, ed. by Donald G. Miller, Browne Barr and Robert S. Paul, 31-42. The Pittsburgh Theological Monograph Series, 36. Pittsburgh: Pickwick Press, 1981.

10.4   Binfield, Clyde. "Principal When Pastor: P. T. Forsyth, 1876-1901." In *The Ministry: Clerical and Lay*, ed. by W. Sheils and Diana Wood, 397-414. London: Basil Blackwell, 1989.

10.5   Binns, J. B. "Peter Taylor Forsyth." In *Report for Sessions 1947-48, New College, London*, 14-18. London: Independent Press, 1948.

10.6   Brown, Robert McAfee. "P. T. Forsyth." In *A Handbook of Christian Theologians*, ed. by D. G. Peerman and Martin E. Marty, 144-165. Cleveland: World Publishing, 1965.

10.7   Cocks, H. F. Lovell. "An Excerpt from the Address Delivered at Commemoration, New College, London, 1977." In *P. T. Forsyth: The Man, the Preachers' Theologian, Prophet for the 20th Century: A Contemporary Assessment*, ed. by Donald G. Miller, Browne Barr and Robert S. Paul, 71-72. The Pittsburgh Theological Monograph Series, 36. Pittsburgh: Pickwick Press, 1981.

The full address is published in New College, London, *Report for Session, 1976-1977*, 8-11.

10.8   ————. "Preface." In *The Church and the Sacraments*, 3d ed., by P. T. Forsyth, vii-xiii. London: Independent Press, 1949.

10.9   Craston, Colin. "The Grace of a Holy God: P. T. Forsyth and the Contemporary Church." In *Authority in the Anglican Communion*, ed. by Stephen W. Sykes, 47-64. Toronto: Anglican Book Centre, 1987.

10.10 Davies, D. R. "Forward." In *The Justification of God: Lectures for War-time on a Christian Theodicy*, 2d ed., by P. T. Forsyth, 5-6. London: Latimer House, 1948.

10.11 Dillistone, F. W. *The Significance of the Cross*. London: Lutterworth Press, 1945.

Portions of the work rely on Forsyth's thought.

10.12 Escott, Harry. "An Appraisement." In *The Cure of Souls: An Appraisement and Anthology of P. T. Forsyth's Practical Writings*, 1-27. Rev. and enl. ed. London: George Allen and Unwin, 1971.

10.13 Garrett, John. "Forsyth, Forsooth." In *Studies of the Church in History: Essays Honoring Robert S. Paul on his 65th Birthday*, ed. by Horton Davies, 243-252. Allison Park, Pa.: Pickwick Publications, 1983.

10.14 Glover, Willis B. *Evangelical Non-Conformists and Higher Criticism in the Nineteenth Century*, 272-282. London: Independent Press, 1954.

10.15   Hunter, A. M. *Teaching and Preaching the New Testament*, 131-187. London: SCM Press, 1963.

10.16   Huxtable, John. "Preface." In *Revelation Old and New: Sermons and Addresses*, [7-8]. London: Independent Press, 1962.

10.17   Johnson, Robert Clyde. *Authority in Protestant Theology*, 100-107. Philadelphia: Westminster Press, 1959.

10.18   Jones, Edgar DeWitt. *The Royalty of the Pulpit*, 128ff. New York: Harper Brothers, 1951.

10.19   Langford, Thomas A. *In Search of Foundations; English Theology, 1900-1920*, 170-175. Nashville: Abingdon Press, 1969.

10.20   Maxwell, Jack M. "A Conversation with Robert Paul." In *Studies of the Church in History: Essays Honoring Robert S. Paul on his 65th Birthday*, ed. by Horton Davies, 3-26. Allison Park, Pa.: Pickwick Publications, 1983.

Discusses Forsyth.

10.21   Mews, Stuart P. "Neo-Orthodoxy, Liberalism and War: Karl Barth, P. T. Forsyth and John Oman, 1914-1918." In *Renaissance and Renewal in Christian History*, ed. by Derek Baker, 361-375. Oxford: Published for the Ecclesiastical History Society by B. Blackwell, 1977.

Papers read at the 15th summer meeting and the 16th winter meeting of the Ecclesiastical History Society.

10.22   Mikolaski, Samuel J. "P. T. Forsyth." In *Creative Minds in Contemporary Theology*, ed. by Philip E. Hughes., 2d rev. ed., 307-340. Grand Rapids: Wm. B. Eerdmans, 1969.

10.23   ————— . "Introduction." In *The Creative Theology of P. T. Forsyth: Selections from His Works*, 7-8. Grand Rapids: Wm. B. Eerdmans, 1969.

10.24   Miller, Donald G. "P. T. Forsyth: The Man." In *P. T. Forsyth; The Man, the Preachers' Theologian, Prophet for the 20th Century: A Contemporary Assessment*, ed. by Donald G. Miller, Browne Barr and Robert S. Paul, 1-29. The Pittsburgh Theological Monograph Series, 36. Pittsburgh: Pickwick Press, 1981.

10.25   Mozley, J. K. "Preface." In *The Church and the Sacraments*, 2d ed., by P. T. Forsyth, vii-xiii. London: Independent Press, 1947.

10.26   ———— . The Heart of the Gospel, chapter 3. London: S.P.C.K., 1925.

10.27   Neill, Stephen. *Twentieth Century Christianity*. London: William Collins & Sons, 1961.

References to *Positive Preaching and the Modern Mind*.

10.28   Paul, Robert S. "Prophet for the Twentieth Century?" In *P. T. Forsyth; The Man, the Preachers' Theologian, Prophet for the 20th Century: A Contemporary Assessment*, ed. by Donald G. Miller, Browne Barr and Robert S. Paul, 43-70.   The Pittsburgh Theological Monograph Series, 36. Pittsburgh: Pickwick Press, 1981.

10.29   ———— . *The Atonement and the Sacraments*, 227-40. New York, Nashville: Abingdon Press, 1960.

Discusses Forsyth's view of the sacraments.

10.30   Peake, A. S. "P. T. Forsyth." In *Recollections and Appreciations,* ed. by W. F. Howard, 192ff. London: Epworth Press, 1938.

10.31   Rodgers, Jack B. and Donald K. McKim.   *The Interpretation and Authority of the Bible*, 393-398. New York: Harper & Row, 1979.

10.32   Rupp, Gordon. "Preface." In *P. T. Forsyth: Per Crucem ad Lucem,* by A. M. Hunter. London: SCM Press, 1974.

Brief comment on Forsyth.

10.33   Thomas, J. Heywood. "Influence on English Thought." In *Legacy and Interpretation of Kierkegaard,* ed. by Niels Thulstrop and M. Mikulova Thulstrop, 160-177. Copenhagen: Reitzel, 1981.

10.34   Vidler, Alec R. *Christian Belief: A Course of Open Lectures Delivered in the University of Cambridge*. London: SCM Press, 1950.

Contains elements of Forsyth's thought.

10.35   Wacker, Grant. "The Dilemmas of Historical Consciousness: The Case of Augustus H. Strong." In *In the Great Tradition: In Honor of Winthrop S. Hudson. Essays on Pluralism, Voluntarism and Revivalism*, ed. by Joseph Ban and Paul R. Dekar, 223-236. Valley Forge: Judson Press, 1982.

Refers to Forsyth.

10.36   Wedel, Theodore O. *The Coming Great Church: Essays on Church Unity*, 70ff. New York: The Macmillan Company, 1945.

Discusses *The Church and the Sacraments*.

10.37   Whale, J. S. "Foreword." In *The Work of Christ*, 2d ed., by P. T. Forsyth, iii-iv. London: Independent Press, 1938.

10.38   Williams, R. R. *Authority in the Apostolic Age, with Two Essays on the Modern Problem of Authority*, 119 ff. London: SCM Press, 1950.

Discusses *The Principle of Authority*.

11. Periodical Articles

11.1   Anderson, Marvin W. "P. T. Forsyth: Prophet of the Cross." *Evangelical Quarterly* 47, no. 3 (July-September 1975): 146-161.

11.2   Barth, Markus. "P. T. Forsyth: The Theologian for the Practical Man." *Congregational Quarterly* 17, no. 4 (October 1939): 436-442.

11.3   Bast, Henry. "Foundations for Preaching." *Reformed Review* 15 (December 1961): 1-18.

Refers to Forsyth's concept of preaching as the "sacramental, saving activity of God."

11.4   Beach, Waldo. "Freedom and Authority in Protestant Ethics." *Journal of Religion* 32 (April 1952): 108-118.

11.5   Bishop, John. "P. T. Forsyth: Preaching and the Modern Mind." *Religion in Life* 48, no. 3 (Autumn 1979): 303-308.

11.6   Bradley, William L. "Forsyth's Contributions to Pastoral Theology." *Religion in Life* 28 no. 4 (Autumn 1959): 546-556.

11.7   Brown, Robert M. "The 'Conversion' of P. T. Forsyth." *Congregational Quarterly* 30 (July 1952): 236-244.

11.8   Caemmerer, R. R. "Why Preach from Biblical Texts–Reflections on Tradition and Practice." *Interpretation* 35, no. 1 (1981): 5-17.

Cites *Positive Preaching and Modern Mind*.

11.9   Camfield, F. W. "Peter Taylor Forsyth." *The Presbyter* 6, no. 2 (1948): 3-10.

11.10   Cave, Sydney. "Dr. Forsyth: 'A Student Tribute.'" *The Christian World* (December 1921): n.p.

11.11   ———. "Dr. P. T. Forsyth: His Influence in Congregationalism." *The Christian World* (24 November 1921): n.p.

11.12   ———. "P. T. Forsyth: The Man and His Writings." *Congregational Quarterly* 26 (April 1948): 107-119.

11.13   Child, R. L. "P. T. Forsyth: Some Aspects of His Thought." *Baptist Times* (3 June 1948): 9.

11.14   Clements, K. W. "Atonement and the Holy Spirit." *Expository Times* 95, no. 6 (1984): 168-171.

Cites *The Work of Christ* and Forsyth's attempt to reconcile the subjective and objective views of the atonement.

11.15   Cocks, H. F. L. "The Message of P. T. Forsyth." *Congregational Quarterly* 26 (July 1948): 214-221.

11.16   ———. "P. T. Forsyth, 'A Voice from a Better Future'." *British Weekly* (6 May 1948): 7.

11.17   Corner, Mark A. "The Umbilical Cord: A View of Man and Nature in the Light of Darwin." *Scottish Journal of Religious Studies* 4, no. 2 (Autumn 1983): 121-137.

Suggests that there are parallels between Darwin's theory of evolution and Forsyth's notion of moral progress.

11.18   Cunliffe-Jones, Hubert. "P. T. Forsyth: Reactionary or Prophet?" *Congregational Quarterly* 28 (October 1950): 344-356.

11.19   Cushman, R. E. "A Study of Freedom and Grace." *Journal of Religion* 25 (1945): 197-212.

11.20   Davies, D. A. "On Re-Reading P. T. Forsyth's *Justification of God*." *British Weekly* (19 October 1939): 31.

11.21   Forster, John. "Dr. Forsyth on the Authority of Grace." *Holborn Review* (April 1907): n.p.

11.22   Garvie, A. E. "A Cross-Centered Theology." *Congregational Quarterly* 22 (1944): 324-330.

11.23   ———. Letter to the editor. *Congregational Quarterly* 12 (1945): 96.

11.24   ———— . "Placarding the Cross: The Theology of P. T. Forsyth." *Congregational Quarterly* (October 1943): 343ff.

11.25   Glegg, Alexander J. Tribute to Forsyth. *The Christian World* (17 November 1921): 4.

11.26   Gossip, A. J. "P. T. Forsyth." *Expository Times* 60 (March 1949): 149.

11.27   Green, Alan. "Personal Memories of P. T. Forsyth." *British Weekly* (13 May 1938): 11.

11.28   Gummer, Selwyn. "Peter Taylor Forsyth: A Contemporary Theologian." *London Quarterly and Holborn Review* 173 (October 1948): 349-353.

Discussion of *The Justification of God.*

11.29   Gunton, C. "Transcendence, Metaphor, and the Knowability of God." *Journal of Theological Studies* 31, no. 8 (1980): 501-516.

Cites *The Person and Place of Jesus Christ.*

11.30   Hamilton, Kenneth. "Created Soul–Eternal Spirit: A Continuing Theological Thorn." *Scottish Journal of Theology* 19, no. 1 (1966): 23-34.

Cites Forsyth's view of the "creaturely nature of man."

11.31   ———— . "Love or Holy Love? Nels Ferré Versus P. T. Forsyth." *Canadian Journal of Theology* 8 (October 1962): 229-236.

11.32   Hanshell, Deryck. "Christian Worship: Catholic and Evangelical." *Downside Review* 90 (301) (1972): 260-267.

Cites Forsyth's view of worship as being "closer to the Roman side than many realize."

11.33   Hermann, E. "Studies of Representative British Theologians: Peter Taylor Forsyth, D.D." *Homiletic Review* 66 (1913): 179-185.

11.34   Higginson, P. T. "The Authentic Word: A Study in Forsyth's Attitude to the Bible." *Churchman* (June 1946): 82-86.

11.35   Hughes, Philip E. "Forsyth: Theologian of the Cross." *Christianity Today* 2 (23 December 1957): 5-7.

11.36   Hughes, T. Hywell. "A Barthian Before Barth?" *Congregational Quarterly* 12 (July 1934): 308-315.

11.37   ———— . "Dr. Forsyth's View of the Atonement." *Congregational Quarterly* 18 (January 1940): 30-37.

11.38   Hunt, G. "Interpreters of Our Faith." *A.D.* (May 1975): 39.

11.39   Hunter, A. M. "P. T. Forsyth Neutestamentler." *Expository Times* 73, no. 4 (January 1962): 100-106.

11.40   Huxtable, John. "National Recognition of Religion." *Congregational Quarterly* 35 (October 1957): 297-310.

Discusses Forsyth and British Free Churches.

11.41   ———— . "Authority." *The Presbyter* 7 (1949): 14-19.

11.42   Jackson, George D. "P. T. Forsyth's Use of the Bible." *Interpretation* 7 (July 1953): 323-337.

11.43   Jenkins, Daniel T. "A Message to Ministers About the Communication of the Gospel." *Theology Today* 6 (July 1949): 174-188.

11.44   Johnson, D. A. "Popular Apologetics in Late-Victorian England–The Work of the Christian Evidence Society." *Journal of Religious History* 11, no. 4 (1981): 558-577.

Cites "Revelation and the Person of Christ" in *Faith and Criticism* (1893).

11.45   Jowett, J. H. "Dr. P. T. Forsyth." *British Weekly* (17 November 1921): 146.

11.46   Kellogg, Edwin H. "A Theologian for the Hour: Peter Taylor Forsyth." *Bulletin of Western Theological Seminary* (April 1914): 5-34.

11.47   Lambert, D. W. "A Great Theologian and His Greatest Book." *London Quarterly and Holborn Review* (July 1948): 244-247.

On *The Person and Place of Jesus Christ*.

11.48   ———— . "The Missionary Message of P. T. Forsyth." *Evangelical Quarterly* 21 (July 1949): 203-208.

11.49   ———— . "The Theology of Missions: The Contribution of P. T. Forsyth." *London Quarterly and Holborn Review* 176 (April 1951): 114-117.

11.50   Lawton, J. S. "Salute to Forsyth." *The Guardian* [Church of England] (18 July n.d.).

11.51 Leembruggen, W. H. "The Witness of P. T. Forsyth – A Theologian of the Cross." *Reformed Theological Review* (1945): 18-46.

11.52 MacKay, John A. "More Light on the Church." *Christian Century* 66 (27 July 1949): 888-890.

11.53 MacKinnon, D. M. "Some Aspects of the Treatment of Christianity by the British Idealists." *Religious Studies* 20, no. 1 (1984): 133-144.

Cites *The Justification of God.*

11.54 Mackintosh, Robert. "The Authority of the Cross." *Congregational Quarterly* 21 (July 1943): 209-218.

11.55 McConnachie, John. "His Work was a Bell Heard Ringing in the Night." *British Weekly* (22 July 1948): 4.

11.56 McMurray Adams, R. H. "Postman's Son Who Became Church Leader." *The Aberdeen Press and Journal* (21 May 1948?): n.p.

11.57 Meadley, Thomas D. "The Forsyth Saga: Fifty Years On." *Methodist Recorder* (11 November 1971): 17.

11.58 ———— . "The Great Church, P. T. Forsyth, and Christian Unity." *London Quarterly and Holborn Review* 190 (July 1965): 225-233.

11.59 ———— . "The 'Obscurity' of P. T. Forsyth." *Congregational Quarterly* 24 (October 1946): 308-317.

11.60 ———— . "A Preacher's Theologian: P. T. Forsyth." *Preacher's and Class-leaders' Magazine* 22 (January-February 1949): 149-153, 157.

11.61 Mikolaski, S. J. "P. T. Forsyth on the Atonement." *Evangelical Quarterly* 36, no. 2 (1964): 78-91.

11.62 ———— . "The Theology of P. T. Forsyth." *Evangelical Quarterly* 36, no. 1 (1964): 27-41.

11.63 Miller, J. S. "Effective Preaching, A Cluster of Conditions." *Scottish Journal of Theology* 36, no. 2 (1983): 229-241.

Cites *Positive Preaching and Modern Mind.*

11.64 "The Missiological Legacy of P. T. Forsyth." *The Japan Christian Quarterly* 51 (Spring 1985): 69-74.

Quotations from *Missions in State and Church* (1908), arranged by O. Bergh.

11.65   Mozley, J. K. "The Theology of Dr. Forsyth." *Expositor* 23 (January 1922): 81-98; (March 1922): 161-181.

Also published in *The Heart of the Gospel*, 66-109. London: S.P.C.K, 1925.

11.66   "Principal Forsyth on 'Wedded Churches.'" *British Congregationalist* (26 February 1914): 156.

Review of an article by Forsyth in the *Daily Chronicle*, 21 February 1914.

11.67   Robinson, N. H. G. "The Importance of P. T. Forsyth." *Expository Times* 64 (December 1952): 76-79.

11.68   Rosenthal, Klaus. "Die Bedeutung des Kreuzesgeschehens für Lehre und Bekenntnis nach Peter Taylor Forsyth." [The Significance of the Event of the Cross for Doctrine and Confession According to P. T. Forsyth.] *Kerygma und Dogma Zeitschrift für Theologische Forschung und Kirchliche Lehre* 7, heft 3 (Juli 1961): 237-259.

11.69   Rowe, Gilbert T. "The Passing of Peter Taylor Forsyth." *Methodist Quarterly Review* 71, no. 1 (January 1922): 162-164.

11.70   Scullard, H. H. "Principal Forsyth." *London Quarterly Review* 137 (January 1922): 104-106.

11.71   Sell, Alan P. F. "Anabaptist-Congregational Relations and Current Mennonite-Reformed Dialogue." *The Mennonite Quarterly Review* 61 (July 1987): 321-334.

11.72   Shaw, J. M. "The Theology of P. T. Forsyth." *Theology Today* 3 (October 1946): 358-370.

11.73   Simpson, A. F. "P. T. Forsyth: The Prophet of Judgment." *Scottish Journal of Theology* 4, no. 2 (1951): 148-156.

11.74   Smith, G. S. "The Spirit of Capitalism Revisited–Calvinists in the Industrial Revolution." *Journal of Presbyterian History* 59 (1981): 481-497.

Cites *Contemporary Review* articles of April and June 1910.

11.75   Surin, K. "Theodicy." *Harvard Theological Review* 76 (1983): 225-247.

Cites *The Justification of God* (1916).

11.76   Swanton, Robert. "Scottish Theology and Karl Barth." *Reformed Theological Review* 33, no. 1 (1974): 17-25.

Barth developed his theology independent of Forsyth.

11.77   Thomas, H. Arnold. "Preachers I Have Known." *Congregational Quarterly* (January 1923): 60.

11.78   Tillich, Paul. "The Present Theological Situation." *Theology Today* 6 (October 1949): 299-310.

11.79   Warschauer, J. "Liberty, Limited: A Rejoinder to Dr. Forsyth." *Contemporary Review* 101 (June 1912): 831-839.

11.80   Webster, D. "P. T. Forsyth's Theology of Missions." *International Review of Missions* 44 (1955): 175-181.

11.81   Wiersbe, W. W. "Theologian for Pastors." *Moody Monthly* (May 1975): 97-101.

11.82   Williams, R. R. "Infant Baptism: Comprehensive or Selective." *Theology* 73 (1970): 99-103.

Cites Forsyth's view of infant baptism.

11.83   Wood, Ralph C. "Christ on Parnassus: P. T. Forsyth Among the Liberals." *Literature and Theology* 2 (March 1988): 83-95.

11.84   Worrall, B. G. "The Authority of Grace in the Theology of P. T. Forsyth." *Scottish Journal of Theology* 25 (February 1972): 58-74.

11.85   ———— . "R. J. Campbell and His New Theology." *Theology* 91 (1978): 342-348.

Cites Forsyth's criticism of Campbell.

11.86   Zeigler, Robert E. "P. T. Forsyth and His Theology." *Methodist Quarterly Review* 62, no. 3 (July 1913): 455-463.

12. Reports in Newspapers

Aberdeen University Review (Aberdeen)

12.1   1921-22, 9: 186. Obituary.

British Congregationalist (London)

12.2   16 January 1908, 51. Forsyth to preach at Mansfield College.

12.3   9 July 1908, 33. His Edinburgh address.

12.4   8 October 1914, 323. His recent illness.

British Weekly (London)

12.5   25 February 1887, 2. "Church Life in Manchester."

12.6   8 March 1894, 322. He accepts call to Cambridge.

12.7   20 September 1894, 364. Begins his ministry at Cambridge.

12.8   4 October 1894, 380. Death of his wife.

12.9   14 April 1898, 492. "Easter Evening"; description of a sermon in Dulwich.

12.10   28 September 1899, 411. Forsyth in Boston.

12.11   5 October 1899, 431, 437. Forsyth in Boston.

12.12   14 February 1901, 459. Forsyth's call to Hackney College.

12.13   7 March 1901, 530. "Dr. P. T. Forsyth of Cambridge," by Lorna (Miss Jane Stoddart).

12.14   21 March 1901, 582. He accepts call to Hackney College.

12.15   21 March 1901, 587. "Dr. Forsyth and Aberdeen," a letter.

12.16   11 April 1901, 664. "Dr. Forsyth in Hackney," a letter.

12.17   12 December 1901, 239. A portrait.

12.18   22 May 1902, 136. Forsyth's resolution on the Education Bill.

12.19   19 June 1902, 242. "Dr. Forsyth at New College."

12.20   17 March 1904, 611. "Principal Forsyth among the Wesleyans."

12.21   12 May 1904, 107ff. Election of Forsyth as Chairman of the Congregational Union; his speech on Chinese labor.

12.22   8 September 1904, 511. "Rev. Dr. Forsyth on Christ's Teaching in Economics."

12.23   18 May 1905, 147. "Dr. Clifford on Principal Forsyth's Address."

12.24   12 October 1905, 3, 4. "Dr. Forsyth's Burden"; a report of Forsyth's address from the Chair of the Union.

12.25   19 October 1905, 35, 36. "Dr. Forsyth's Plea to the Archbishops"; "Dr. Forsyth on Passive Resistance."

12.26   26 October 1905, 59. "The Bishop of Bristol and Dr. Forsyth."

12.27   19 April 1906, 31. Interview with Forsyth on the Education Bill.

12.28   10 May 1906, 104. Forsyth at the Assembly.

12.29   19 July 1906, 370. "Dr. Forsyth," a letter.

12.30   4 October 1906, 617. "The Correspondence of Claudius Clear," a report of Forsyth's Aberdeen University sermon.

12.31   29 November 1906, 211. "The Congregational Union and the Education Bill," quotes Forsyth's address.

12.32   14 March 1907, 634. "Dr. Forsyth's Position," a letter. "The Leicester Conference and the New Theology," a letter.

12.33   25 April 1907, 57ff. "Principal Forsyth's Impressions of America."

12.34   17 March 1910, 480. Forsyth's address at the National Free Church Council.

12.35   12 May 1910, 132. R. J. Campbell's reference to Forsyth at the Assembly.

12.36   19 October 1911, 90. The contention between Forsyth and Campbell.

12.37   2 November 1911, 132. "Dr. Forsyth and Mr. Campbell," two letters.

12.38   9 November 1911, 170. Three further letters about their disagreement.

12.39   16 November 1911, 196. Another five letters on the disagreement.

12.40   4 September 1913, 549. "Principal Forsyth: The Roosevelt of Modern Theology."

12.41   19 March 1914, 730. "Dr. Forsyth's Address at Norwich."

12.42   11 November 1915, 108. "Dr. Forsyth and Mr. Campbell," a letter.

12.43   16 November 1916, 128. "Principal Forsyth at Westminster Chapel."

12.44   17 November 1921, 162-163. "A Personal Tribute," by J. K. Mozley.

12.45   17 November 1921, 148. "Memorial Service for Dr. Forsyth."

12.46   17 November 1921, 145. "Principal Forsyth," by W. R. Nicoll.

12.47   17 November 1921, 162. "Principal Forsyth, A Memoir."

12.48   17 November 1921, 146, 153-154. "Tributes to Dr. Forsyth," by T. H. Darlow, J. H. Jowett, H. T. Andrews, Principal Selbie, Alex Souter, and T. Charles Williams.

12.49   24 November 1921, 185. "More Tributes to Principal Forsyth," by W. S. Bruce, S. Maurice Watts, W. E. Blomfield, and T. R. Grantham.

12.50   24 November 1921, 196. Letter, "Principal Forsyth," by H. Vincent Ruhu, a letter.

12.51   1 December 1921, 203. Letter, "A Medical Man's Tribute to Dr. Forsyth," a letter.

12.52   18 May 1922, 141. "Memorial tablet to Dr. Forsyth unveiled at Hackney College."

The Christian World (London)

12.53   17 November 1921, 3. "Death of Principal Forsyth."

The Congregational Monthly (London)

12.54   March 1888, 1: 64. Mention of an address by Forsyth.

12.55   June 1888, 1: 180. Forsyth's call to Leicester.

12.56   July 1888, 1: 201. Forsyth's address noted.

12.57   October 1892, 5: 289. Mention of an address by Forsyth on the growth of population in large towns.

12.58   February 1893, 6: 51. Forsyth appointed College Pastor at Oxford.

12.59   December 1893, 6: 326. Forsyth appointed to Leicester Museum and Art Gallery Committee.

12.60   March 1894, 7: 93. Forsyth accepts call to Cambridge.

12.61   September 1899, 12: 205. Forsyth sails for Boston.

12.62   April 1900, n.s. 1: 8. Aphorism quoted.

12.63   April 1901, n.s. 1: 3. Forsyth accepts call to Hackney College.

12.64   July 1901, n.s. 2: 3. Forsyth's address at Lancashire Independent College.

12.65   October 1903, n.s. 4: 229. "Peter Taylor Forsyth, The Life-Story of the Principal of Hackney College."

12.66   June 1905, n.s. 5: 107. "P. T. Forsyth, M.A., D.D., The New Chairman of the Congregational Union."

Literary Digest (London)

12.67   23 August 1913, 288-289. "The Roosevelt of Modern Theology." Includes portrait.

Manchester Examiner and Times (Manchester)

12.68   23 January 1888, 7. "Ministers and the Sunday Question." Report of a sermon delivered by Forsyth at Cheetham Hill Congregational Church.

The Outlook (London)

12.69   2 September 1899, 55. Article mentions Forsyth; includes portrait.

The Times (London)

12.70   26 February 1906, 12. Accepts Lyman Beecher Lectureship.

12.71   9 March 1906, 10. At Birmingham, "Evangelical Free Churches Council." On the place of spiritual experience in the making of theology.

12.72   28 November 1906, 7. At City Temple, on Education Bill.

12.73   13 February 1909, 9. At University College, "The Study of the Bible."

12.74   15 April 1909, 5. Appointed vice-chairman of London Congregational Board of Ministers.

12.75 14 May 1909, 7. At Congregational Union Conference on Christianity.

12.76 14 October 1909, 4. At Sheffield, on modernism.

12.77 11 March 1910, 4. At "The Free Church Council."

12.78 28 April 1910, 4. At Bloomsbury Chapel, "The Baptist Anniversaries."

12.79 10 March 1911, 4. At Evangelical Free Church Conference, "Free Church Council, Religious Reunion."

12.80 12 October 1911, 12. At Congregational Union Conference on Christianity.

12.81 4 October 1913, 8. At Southhampton, "Church Congress, Problems of Property and Rural Life."

12.82 13 May 1914, 6. At Memorial Hall, "Church and Nation, Dr. Forsyth on Spiritual Independence."

12.83 10 October 1914, 11. His health.

12.84 9 May 1918, 3. At Memorial Hall, "Christian Union, Dr. Forsyth on a New Phase."

12.85 12 October 1919, 12. At Congregational Union Conference.

12.86 12 November 1921, 14. "Death of Principal Forsyth, an Original Thinker."

12.87 16 November 1921, 13. Description of Forsyth's funeral.

12.88 25 March 1922, 12. His will.

13. Reviews of Books and Articles

Reviews of Forsyth's Writings

The Charter of the Church

13.1 *British Weekly* (21 May 1896): 65ff.

13.2 *London Quarterly Review* (January 1897): 205ff.

13.3 *Presbyterian and Reformed Review* 7 (1896): 757. By B. B. Warfield.

Christ on Parnassus

13.4   *Church Quarterly Review* (October 1912): 226ff.

13.5   *Church Quarterly Review* 162 (July-September 1961): 387-388. By G. Cope.

13.6   *Expository Times* 23 (November 1911): 74. By Charles W. Hodge.

13.7   *Times Literary Supplement* (5 October 1911): 371.

The Christian Ethic of War

13.8   *Ethics* 27 (1916-17): 399.

13.9   *Expository Times* 28 (November 1916): 55. By Edwin H. Kellogg.

13.10 *Times Literary Supplement* 15 (1916): 426.

13.11 *Times Literary Supplement* (24 August 1916): 408.

Christian Perfection

13.12 *London Quarterly Review* (April 1899): 383.

The Church and the Sacraments

13.13 *Bibliotheca Sacra* 74 (1912): 638-639. By W. H. Griffith-Thomas.

13.14 *Expository Times* 28 (August 1917): 497-498. By Edwin H. Kellogg.

13.15 *Journal of Theological Studies* 19 (October 1917): 91-94. By Harold Hamilton.

13.16 *London Quarterly and Holborn Review* (January 1910): 145.

13.17 *London Quarterly and Holborn Review* (October 1948): 377.

13.18 *London Quarterly Review* (July 1917): 131ff.

13.19 *Methodist Review* 101 (May 1918): 462-464.

13.20 *Times Literary Supplement* (24 May 1917): 251.

The Church, the Gospel and Society

13.21   *Modern Churchman*, n.s. 6 (April 1963): 245-246. By R. Preston.

Congregationalism and Reunion

13.22   *Baptist Quarterly* 15 (January 1953): 46-47. By G. W. Hughes.

The Cruciality of the Cross

13.23   *Baptist Quarterly* 13 (January 1949): 44-45. By R. L. Child.

13.24   *Expository Times* 21 (November 1909): 84.

13.25   *Faith and Mission* 1, no. 2 (Spring 1984): 86-87. By L. B. Smith.

13.26   *London Quarterly Review* 113 (January 1910): 145.

Faith and Criticism

13.27   *London Quarterly Review* (October 1893): 1ff.

13.28   *Presbyterian and Reformed Review* 5 (1894): 354-356. By B. B. Warfield.

Faith, Freedom, and the Future

13.29   *Congregational Quarterly* 36 (October 1958): 270. By J. Huxtable.

13.30   *Expository Times* (June 1912): 411ff.

13.31   *Expository Times* 67 (April 1956): 202-203. By C. S. Duthie.

13.32   *Journal of Theological Studies* 15 (1913): 132ff.

13.33   *Religion in Life* 26, no. 2 (Spring 1957): 310-312. By William L. Bradley.

13.34   *Times Literary Supplement* (21 March 1912): 119.

God the Holy Father

13.35   *The Christian World* (14 December 1978): n.p.

13.36   *Methodist Recorder* (18 January 1979): 6. By Frank Cumbers.

The Holy Father and the Living Christ

13.37   *Expository Times* (April 1898): 269.

The Justification of God

13.38   *Anglican Theological Review* 35 (January 1953): 63-64. By F. W. Dillistone.

13.39   *Boston Transcript* (12 September 1917): 6.

13.40   *Expository Times* (January 1917): 177.

13.41   *Journal of Bible and Religion* 20 (January 1952): 44-45. By J. Gardner.

13.42   *Methodist Review* 99 (July 1917): 650-653.

13.43   *New York Times* (25 November 1917): 500.

13.44   *Times Literary Supplement* (23 November 1916): 564.

Marriage, Its Ethic and Religion

13.45   *Ethics* 24 (1913-14): 115.

13.46   *Expository Times* (November 1912): 79.

13.47   *Methodist Quarterly Review* 62, no. 3 (July 1913): 609. By Mary Helm.

13.48   *Princeton Theological Review* 11 (1913): 546-548. By William B. Green.

Missions in State and Church

13.49   *British Weekly* (15 October 1908): 50.

13.50   *Church Quarterly Review* (April 1910): 208.

13.51   *Expository Times* 20 (November 1908): 86. By B. B. Warfield.

The Old Faith and the New

13.52   *Congregational Monthly* 4 (December 1891): 320ff.

The Person and Place of Jesus Christ

13.53   *American Journal of Theology* 14 (April 1910): 313ff. By C. A. Exley.

13.54   *Bibliotheca Sacra* 67 (1910): 363-364. By Charles W. Hodge.

13.55   *British Weekly* (21 October 1909): 57ff.

13.56   *Expository Times* 21 (April 1910): 320. By Arthur Boutwood.

13.57   *Expository Times* 64 (April 1953): 195-198. By H. F. L. Cocks.

13.58   *Hibbert Journal* 8 (May 1910): 686-690. By Arthur Boutwood.

13.59   *Independent* (28 July 1910): 197ff.

13.60   *Journal of Theological Studies* 12 (1911): 298-300. By J. K. Mozley.

13.61   *Methodist Quarterly Review* 59, no. 3 (July 1910): 618-621. By
        A. J. Lamar.

13.62   *Nation* (20 October 1910): 367ff.

13.63   *New York Times* (16 July 1910): 400ff.

13.64   *Princeton Theological Review* 7 (1910): 688-693. By Charles W. Hodge.

13.65   *Theology* 42 (April 1941): 229-235. By J. K. Mozley.

Positive Preaching and Modern Mind

13.66   *Baptist Quarterly* 13 (October 1949): 190-191. By I. J. Barnes.

13.67   *Biblical World* 31 (May 1908): 400.

13.68   *British Weekly* (24 October 1907): 57ff. By James Denney.

13.69   *Concordia Journal* 7 (November 1981): 260-261. By F. C. Rossow.

13.70   *Expository Times* 72 (August 1961): 324-326. By F. D. Coggan.

13.71   *Independent* (20 August 1908): 436.

13.72   *London Quarterly Review* (January 1908): 1ff.

13.73   *Methodist Review* 90 (May 1908): 491-492.

13.74   *Modern Churchman* 40 (June 1950): 166-167. By W. G. Fallows.

13.75   *Nation* (26 March 1908): 284.

13.76   *New York Times* (9 May 1908): 267.

13.77   *Outlook* (7 March 1908): 560.

13.78   *Princeton Theological Review* 7 (1909): 519-521. By C. P. Erdmon.

13.79   *Public Opinion* (May 1949): 333.

13.80   *Saturday Review* 106 (4 July 1908): 24.

13.81   *Springfielder* 30 (Spring 1966): 67-69. By G. Aho.

13.82   *The Presbyter* 7 (1949): 27-28. By S. B. Harris.

13.83   *Times Literary Supplement* 6 (19 December 1907): 387.

The Principle of Authority

13.84   *Baptist Quarterly* 14 (October 1952): 378-379. By A. W. Argyle.

13.85   *Congregational Quarterly* 31 (January 1953): 75-76. By H. F. Lovell Cocks.

13.86   *Expository Times* 24 (February 1913): 213. By J. Warschauer.

13.87   *Hibbert Journal* 12 (July 1914): 936-941. By A. R. Whatley.

13.88   *London Quarterly Review* (April 1913): 340ff.

13.89   *London Quarterly and Holborn Review* 172 (October 1947): 316-324. By H. Cunliffe-Jones.

13.90   *Methodist Quarterly Review* 62, no. 3 (July 1913): 587-588. By Delo C. Grover.

13.91   *Princeton Theological Review* 12 (1914): 125-127. By George Johnson.

Religion in Recent Art

13.92   *London Quarterly Review* (January 1902): 201.

13.93   *New York Times* (7 June 1902): 379.

13.94   *Outlook* 72 (25 October 1902): 463-464.

Rome, Reform and Reaction

13.95   *British Weekly* (11 January 1900): 306.

13.96   *London Quarterly Review* (April 1900): 352.

The Soul of Prayer

13.97   *London Quarterly Review* (January 1917): 130ff.

The Taste of Death and the Life of Grace

13.98   *Expository Times* (June 1901): 367.

Theology in Church and State

13.99   *American Journal of Theology* 20 (1916): 615ff. By F. A. Starratt.

13.100 *Biblical World* 47 (1916): 341-342. By Edwin H. Kellogg.

13.101 *Boston Transcript* (17 June 1916): 6.

13.102 *Congregational Quarterly* 35 (October 1957): 297-310. By J. Huxtable.

13.103 *Expository Times* 27 (May 1916): 276-277.

13.104 *Methodist Quarterly Review* 65, no. 3 (October 1916): 782-785. By H. M. DuBose.

13.105 *Methodist Review* 98 (September 1916): 816-818.

13.106 *New York Times* (6 August 1916): 312.

13.107 *Springfield Republican* (5 March 1916): 15.

13.108 *Times Literary Supplement* 14 (30 December 1915): 495.

This Life and the Next

13.109 *American Library Association Booklist* 14 (1918): 313.

13.110   *Baptist Quarterly* 13 (January 1949): 44-45. By R. L. Child.

13.111   *Biblical World* 53 (1919): 204. By W. H. Griffith-Thomas.

13.112   *Bibliotheca Sacra* 75 (1918): 604-607. By W. H. Griffith-Thomas.

13.113   *Bookman* 47 (1918): 653. By Tertius Van Dyke.

13.114   *Boston Transcript* (24 August 1918): 3. By Tertius Van Dyke.

13.115   *London Quarterly Review* (April 1918): 121.

13.116   *Methodist Review* 101 (September 1918): 807-810.

13.117   *Springfield Republican* (27 August 1918): 6.

13.118   *Times Literary Supplement* 17 (September 1918): 175.

13.119   *Times Literary Supplement* (11 April 1918): 175.

The Work of Christ

13.120   *Expository Times* (November 1910): 84.

13.121   *Expository Times* 59 (1947): 92. By R. W. Stewart.

13.122   *London Quarterly Review* 115 (January 1911): 151.

13.123   *London Quarterly Review* 173 (July 1948): 244-247. By D. W. Lambert.

Reviews of Writings Relating to Forsyth

The Creative Theology of P. T. Forsyth (Mikolaski)

13.124   *Christianity Today* 13 (1 August 1969): 16. By W. C. Robinson.

13.125   *Evangelical Quarterly* 42 (1970): 247-248. By A. S. Wood.

13.126   *Journal of the American Academy of Religion* 38 (September 1970): 342-343. By C. A. McKay, Jr.

13.127   *Reformed Review* 23 (Fall 1969): 29-30. By W. H. Bos.

13.128   *Westminster Theological Journal* 33 (November 1970): 111-112. By A. M. Harman.

The Gospel and Authority: A P. T. Forsyth Reader (Anderson)

13.129   *Choice* 9 (1972): 660.

13.130   *Expository Times* 84 (November 1972): 57-58. By Allan D. Galloway.

13.131   *Lutheran Quarterly* 24 (May 1972): 210-212. By P. H. Pfatteicher.

P. T. Forsyth: The Man and His Work (Bradley)

13.132   *Church Quarterly Review* 153 (1952): 516-520. By W. F. Lofthouse.

13.133   *Congregational Quarterly* 31 (January 1953): 73-74. By S. Cave.

13.134   *Interpretation* 8 (October 1954): 490-491. By C. Gamble.

13.135   *Religion in Life* 22, no. 3 (Summer 1953): 469-470. By Lynn H. Hough.

P. T. Forsyth: The Man, the Preachers' Theologian (Miller)

13.136   *Expository Times* 94 (March 1983): 184. By D. W. C. Ford.

P. T. Forsyth: Per Crucem ad Lucem (Hunter)

13.137   *Anglican Theological Review* 59 (July 1977): 349-350. By F. M. McClain.

13.138   *Church History* 44 (June 1975): 274-275. By Neal C. Gillespie.

13.139   *Perkins School of Theology Journal* 29 (Winter 1976): 45-46. By Geoffrey D. Scott.

13.140   *Theology* 77 (October 1974): 544-545. By B. G. Worrall.

P. T. Forsyth, Prophet for Today (Brown)

13.141   *Interpretation* 8 (January 1954): 99-100. By K. B. Cully.

13.142   *Religion in Life* 22, no. 3 (Summer 1953): 469-470. By Lynn H. Hough.

13.143   *Scottish Journal of Theology* 9 (December 1956): 447. By G. W. Bromiley.

13.144   *Theology Today* 10 (October 1953): 429-431. By J. M. Shaw.

The Theology of P. T. Forsyth (Griffith)

13.145 *Theology Today* 7 (July 1950): 268-269. By J. N. Thomas.

The Theology of P. T. Forsyth (Rodgers)

13.146 *Canadian Journal of Theology* 12 (April 1966): 141-142. By R. F. Aldwinckle.

13.147 *Christian Century* 82 (6 October 1965): 1230f. By D. O. Woodyard.

13.148 *Christianity Today* 9 (25 September 1965): 20-21. By J. Daane.

13.149 *Churchman* 80 (March 1966): 49-50. By J. P. Baker.

13.150 *Expository Times* 77 (June 1966): 268-269. By D. Ebor.

13.151 *Journal of Religious Thought* 23, no. 2 (1966-1967): 187-188. By J. D. Roberts.

13.152 *Journal of Theological Studies*, n.s. 18 (April 1967): 288-289. By N. H. G. Robinson.

13.153 *London Quarterly and Holborn Review* 191 (April 1966): 164-165. By Frederic Greeves.

14. Theses and Dissertations

Theses

14.1 Brasington, Edwin C. "A Presentation of the Christology of Peter Taylor Forsyth." Th.M. thesis, Union Theological Seminary in Virginia, 1954. xiii, 129 pp.

14.2 Caldwell, David R. "Revelation and Authority in P. T. Forsyth." Th.M. thesis, Southern Baptist Theological Seminary, 1959. iii, 90 pp.

14.3 Cumbie, Charles R. "The Social Ethics of Peter Taylor Forsyth." Th.M. thesis, Southern Baptist Theological Seminary, 1960. xi, 97 pp.

14.4 Dail, Frances R. "Peter Taylor Forsyth's Conception of the Person and Work of Christ." B.D. thesis, Duke University, 1947. 98 pp.

14.5   Ekerholm, David L. "British Kenoticism: A Comparison of the Kenotic Christologies of Andrew Martin Fairbairn and Peter Taylor Forsyth." M.A. thesis, Trinity Evangelical Divinity School, 1978. vi, 94 pp.

14.6   Fleming, Deryl. "Towards a Theology of Worship from a Free Church Perspective." D.Min. thesis, Wesley Theological Seminary, 1984. 155 pp.

Forsyth's work is cited as an example of worship in the free church tradition.

14.7   Frazier, Thomas Richard. "American Reactions to P. T. Forsyth." M.A. thesis, Southern Methodist University, 1953. iv, 104 pp.

14.8   Lawler, Howard L. "The Universalism of P. T. Forsyth: An Exposition to Indicate Particular Problems." M.A. thesis, Wheaton College, 1987. vi, 153 pp.

14.9   Roberts, Joseph A. "The Atonement in P. T. Forsyth." Th.M. thesis, Southern Baptist Theological Seminary, 1956. 57 pp.

14.10 Thompson, Douglass Brian. "The Christology of P. T. Forsyth: A Preliminary Study." Th.M. thesis, Princeton Theological Seminary, 1950. v, 110 pp.

14.11 Thompson, E. Eugene. "The Contribution of P. T. Forsyth to New Testament Theology." S.T.M. thesis, Oberlin College, 1949. ii, 133 pp.

14.12 Tietge, Theodore A. "Doxological Preaching." Thesis, Wesley Theological Seminary, 1978. ix, 201 pp.

Discusses Forsyth.

Dissertations

14.13 Allen, Ray. "The Christology of P. T. Forsyth." Duke University, 1953. 320 pp.

14.14 Bradley, W. L. "The Theology of P.T. Forsyth, 1848-1921." University of Edinburgh, 1949.

Published as *P. T. Forsyth, the Man and His Work*. London: Independent Press, 1952. The dissertation includes an excellent bibliography of Forsyth's articles, which was omitted from the book.

14.15   Brown, Robert M. "P. T. Forsyth and the Gospel of Grace." Columbia University, 1951. vii, 746 pp.

Published as *P. T. Forsyth: Prophet for Today*. Philadelphia: Westminster Press, 1952.

14.16   Gardner, Harry M. "The Doctrine of the Person and Work of Jesus Christ in the Thought of Peter Taylor Forsyth and of Emil Brunner." Boston University, 1962. vi, 371 pp.

14.17   Hsu, John Dao-Luong. "Peter Taylor Forsyth's Concept of Spirituality." Aquinas Institute of Theology, 1974. v, 237 pp.

14.18   Jackson, George D. "The Biblical Basis of the Theology of P. T. Forsyth." Princeton Theological Seminary, 1952. iv, 455 pp.

14.19   Kelley, Jeffrey O. "The Gospel of God's Grace as the Locus of Authority in the Free Church Tradition: A Critical Evaluation of the Thought of Peter Taylor Forsyth." University of Chicago, 1987. ii, 121 pp.

14.20   McKay, Clifford A., Jr. "The Moral Structure of Reality in the Theology of Peter Taylor Forsyth." Vanderbilt University, 1970. 323 pp.

14.21   Newman, Guy D. "The Theology of P. T. Forsyth with Special Reference to His Christology." Southwestern Baptist Theological Seminary, 1953. 204 pp.

14.22   Parker, Gary E. "A Comparison of the Concept of Proclamation in the Writings of Peter Taylor Forsyth and Rudolf Bultmann." Baylor University, 1984. viii, 232 pp.

14.23   Pitt, C. S. "Church, Ministry and Sacraments: A Critical Evaluation of the Thought of Peter Taylor Forsyth." New College, London, 1977.

Published as *Church, Ministry and Sacraments: A Critical Evaluation of the Thought of Peter Taylor Forsyth*. Washington, D.C.: University Press of America, 1983.

14.24   Rosser, William R. "The Cross of Christ as the Hermeneutical Norm for Scriptural Interpretation in the Theology of Peter Taylor Forsyth." Southern Baptist Theological Seminary, 1990. viii, 259 pp.

14.25   Simpson, A. F. "Certainty Through Faith: An Examination of the Religious Philosophy of Peter Taylor Forsyth." New College, London, 1949.

14.26   Stewart, Winthrop R. "The Biblical Foundations and Insights of P. T. Forsyth's Theology." Aberdeen, 1965.

14.27   Thompson, Robert F. "Peter Taylor Forsyth: A Pre-Barthian." Drew University, 1940. 255 pp.

14.28   Wilson, Reginald A. "The Problem of Religious Authority in Contemporary Theological Thought with Special Reference to the Interpretations of John Oman, P. T. Forsyth, and A. E. J. Rawlinson." Columbia University, 1960. xii, 374 pp.

14.29   Wismar, Don R. "A Sacramental View of Preaching as Seen in the Writings of John Calvin and P. T. Forsyth and Applied to the Mid-Twentieth Century." Pacific School of Religion, 1963. vi, 251 pp.

15. Unpublished Papers and Records

15.1   McKim, Donald K. "The Authority of Scripture in P. T. Forsyth." Pittsburgh, 1973. [20 pp.] The Library, Union Theological Seminary in Virginia.

15.2-   New College Library, London.
15.12   New College, University of London, ceased to exist in 1977, but continues as a foundation which helps theological students preparing for ministry. See entries below.

15.2   File 182/3/2/1. Letter from J. F. Andrews to J. B. Binns regarding Forsyth, 7 October 1948.

15.3   File 182/3/2/2. Letter from J. F. Andrews to J. B. Binns regarding Forsyth, 10 October 1948.

15.4   File 182/3/2/4. Letter from J. F. Andrews to Dr. Cave regarding Forsyth, 30 June 1948.

15.5   File 182/3/2/5. Letter from J. F. Andrews to J. B. Binns regarding Forsyth, 13 October 1948.

15.6   File 182/3/9. References to Forsyth's health in minutes of New College, London.

15.7   File 182/3/12. References to Forsyth's health in minutes of New College, London.

15.8   File 244/2. Midsummer examination in Apologetics, set by Forsyth, 1902.

15.9   File 536/22. Letter to Forsyth from J. K. Mozley, 20 January 1909.

15.10 Forsyth's letter from Gwalia Hotel in Llandrindod Wells, Wales to James Shepheard of Lyndhurst Rd., Congregational Church, saying he could not give an address because of the pressure of work, 23 July 1913.

15.11 "The Addresses delivered at the unveiling of the Tablet erected in the College Library, to the memory of–Rev. Peter Taylor Forsyth," 11 May 1922.

15.12 Program for 275th Commemoration of the founding of the Harmondsworth Charity (which later became New College, London) containing a reference to Forsyth as a "most distinguished alumnus" of New College, 10 June 1948.

15.13 Price, Charles. "Introduction to the Theology of P. T. Forsyth." Notes of lectures given at the Protestant Episcopal Theological Seminary in Alexandria, Virginia, 1960.

II
SOURCE INDEX FOR
PRINCIPAL WORKS

SCRIPTURE INDEX

See the abbreviations on pages xvii and xviii for a complete list of works on which the indexing is based.

Gospels *(continued)*

Sermon on the Mount

Sermon on the Mount *(continued)*

Epistles

Matthew

INDEX OF NAMES
AND CITED WORKS

See the abbreviations on pages xvii and xviii for a complete list of works on which the indexing is based.

Abel (OT), **COC**: 84
Abijah (OT), **RRR**: 28
Abraham (OT), **MSC**: 302; **WOC**: 12; **COP**: 248-249; **FFF**: 308; **SOP**: 86; **CAS**: 46, 71; **GHF**: 89; **CGS-HC**: 53
Acton, John Emerich Edward Dalberg, **FFF**: 158
Adam (OT), **CAS**: 106; **GHF**: 42
Addison, Joseph, "Dream of Mirza," **CAS**: 299
Adolphus, Gustavus, **SOP**: 49; **CAS**: 55
Aeschylus, **PPMM**: 227; **COP**: 14, 29, 36
Oedipus, **COP**: 16
Ahijah (OT), **CAS**: 228
Aholiab, see Oholiab (OT)
Alden, Percy, **MSC**: 36
Alexander the Great, **RRA**: 2
Alfred, King, **CGS-GG**: 79
Alva, **PPJC**: 4; **FFF**: 135
Ambrose, **COC**: 80; **TCS**: 320
Amiel, **PPMM**: 156
Amos (OT), **TCS**: 321
Andrews, Herbert Tom, **TCS**: x; **CAS**: 153
Angelico, Fra, **COTC**: 31; **COP**: 79, 147
Angelico, Francis, **COTC**: 31

Anselm of Canterbury, **PPMM**: 199, 253; **COTC**: 96; **PPJC**: 21, 246; **WOC**: 47, 223, 232; **COP**: 99-100, 182; **POA**: 330; **TCS**: 280
Apuleius, **CAS**: 168
Aquinas, Thomas, **RRA**: [1]; **COC**: 87, 92; **RRR**: 181; **PPMM**: 11; **COP**: 179; **TCS**: 280; **CAS**: 41
Aristophanes, **PPMM**: 88; **COP**: 36; **JOG**: 204
Clouds, **COP**: 90
Aristotle, **RRA**: 87; **PPMM**: 81-82, 207; **PPJC**: 290, 312; **COP**: 23; **FFF**: 99, 106; **GHF**: 84, 121
Arius, **POA**: 218
Arnold, Matthew, **RRR**: 181, 239; **PPMM**: 88; **COP**: 247; **CAS**: 279; **GHF**: 52, 123; **CGS-GG**: 100
"Stanzas from the Grande Chartreuse," **GHF**: 88
Arthur, King, **CAS**: 301
Athanasius, **RRR**: 14; **PPMM**: 80, 82; **COTC**: 79; **PPJC**: 246; **POA**: 218, 173; **TCS**: 280; **CAR-RR**: 27; **CGS-HC**: 20
Augustine of Canterbury, **MSC**: 267, 314

Boniface I, Pope, **CAS**: 79
Boniface, Saint, **MSC**: 38, 314
Booth, **MSC**: 23
Borgeaud, Charles,
 The Rise of Modern Democracy in Old and New England (1894), **FFF**: 106
Bossuet, Jacques-Bénigne, **JOG**: 26
Botticelli, Sandro, **RRA**: 21, 66
Bousset, Wilhelm, **PPJC**: 11, 79, 105, 275
Bradford, Amory H., **RRR**: v
Bradlaugh, Charles, **PPJC**: 5
Bridgewater Treatises, **JOG**: 140
Bright, John, **CEW**: 81
Bright, William, **COP**: 296
Brontë, Emily Jane,
 Wuthering Heights, **PPJC**: 241
Brown, **COP**: 279
Brown, John,
 Apostolic Succession in the Light of History and Fact (1898), **RRR**: vii
Brown, William Adams,
 Christian Theology in Outline (1906), **PPMM**: 182-183
Browne, Robert, **FFF**: 136, 346
Browning, [Elizabeth Barrett?] Mrs.,
 "Drama of Exile," **RRA**: 140
Browning, Robert, **RRA**: 175; **PPMM**: 5, 236; **PPJC**: 193; **WOC**: 16-18; **COP**: 200; **FFF**: 172, 246; **JOG**: 135; **CAS**: 50; **CGS-GG**: 121
 "Abt Vogler," **COP**: 245
 "Apparent Failure," **GHF**: 91
 "Epistle ot Karshish," **RRA**: 300; **FFF**: 6-7
 "Johannes Agricola in Meditation," **COP**: 183
 "Love among the Ruins," **RRA**: 62
 The Ring and the Book, **GHF**: 37
 "The Statue and the Bust," **COP**: 285
Bruce, Alexander Balmain, **CAS**: 153-156, 158
 Apologetics; or, Christianity Defensively Stated (1892), **JOG**: 224
 The Providential Order of the World (1897), **JOG**: 224

Buccleuch, Duke of, **CAS**: 180
Buckle, [Henry Thomas?], **JOG**: 46
Buddha, **PPJC**: 43, 241, 254; **POA**: 207, 327
Bunsen, Christian Karl Josias, Freiherr von, **RRR**: viii, 45
 God in History; or The Progress of Man's Faith in the Moral Order of the World (1860; Eng. trans., 1868-1870), **JOG**: 34, 40-41
Bunyan, John, **FFF**: 143; **POA**: 287
 Pilgrim's Progress, **FFF**: 144; **CAS**: 299
Burke, Edmund, **SCP**: 12; **POA**: 235, 245; **CEW**: 12; **CAS**: 228; **CAR-RR**: 34
Burne Jones, Edward, **RRA**: 49ff, 97, 154, 99-100
 "Song of Love," **RRA**: 31
 "Pygmalion," **RRA**: 123
Burns, Cecil Delisle, **CEW**: 64
 Political Ideals, Their Nature and Development: An Essay (1915), **CEW**: 110
Burns, Robert, **COP**: 59, 146; **MER**: 60; **TLTN**: 59
Burroughs, Canon, **CAR-RR**: 27
Burroughs, Jeremiah,
 Irenicum, to the Lovers of Truth and Peace . . . (1653), **FFF**: 332
Butler, Joseph, **PPJC**: 256
 The Analogy of Religion, Natural and Revealed, to the Constitution and Course of Nature, 4th ed. (1890), **JOG**: 224
Buxton, Thomas Fowell, **MSC**: 192
Byron, George Noel Gordon, **RRA**: 33; **PPMM**: 156; **JOG**: 134

Cadbury, George, **MSC**: 176
Caesar, Gaius Julius, **JOG**: 205
Caiaphas (NT), **PPJC**: 161; **CEW**: 95
Cain (OT), **COC**: 84; **TLTN**: 10, 12
Caligula, Gaius Caesar Augustus Germanicus, **FFF**: 153
Calvin, John, **RRA**: 250; **COC**: 89, 91; **RRR**: 29, 139; **PPMM**: 93, 98, 112;

Dale, Thomas Pelham,
The Life and Letters of Thomas Pelham Dale (1894), **FFF**: 177
Dalman, Gustaf Hermann, **PPJC**: 275
Dante Alighieri, **RRA**: [1], 11, 19, 26, 30, 32, 161, 224; **COC**: 40, 87; **PPMM**: 244; **MSC**: 32; **COP**: 20, 77, 125, 179; **GHF**: 73, 84
Divine Comedy, **COP**: 236, 251; **JOG**: 16, 76
Paradiso, **SOP**: 90
Darwin, Charles, **PPJC**: 145
David (OT), **COTC**: 88; **COP**: 66, 70; **CGS-GG**: 113
Davidson, Andrew Bruce,
The Book of Job (1884), **JOG**: 224
Davidson, [John?], **PPJC**: 248
Dawson, George,
Prayers with a Discourse on Prayer (1882), **SOP**: 76
Demosthenes, **PPMM**: 2
Denck, Hans, **FFF**: 131
Denney, James, **TCS**: 33
Dexter, Henry Martyn, **FFF**: 170
Dickens, Charles, **MSC**: 128; **JOG**: 114; **CAS**: 259; **GHF**: 6
Dicksee, Frank,
Harmony, **RRA**: 68
Didache, **COC**: 52; **CAS**: 271
Dieterich, Albrecht,
Eine Mithrasliturgie [Liturgy of Mithras] (1903), **CAS**: 168
Döllinger, Johann Joseph Ignaz von, **COC**: 12; **POA**: 282
Drews, Arthur, *see* Hegel, Georg Wilhelm Friedrich
Drinkwater, John, **CAR-RR**: 30
Drummond, Henry,
Natural Law in the Spiritual World (1883), **MSC**: 167
du Maurier, George Louis Palmella Busson, **COP**: 276
Punch, **RRA**: 17
Duns Scotus, John, **POA**: 163, 394; **TCS**: 67
Dürer, Albrecht, **PPMM**: 226; **COP**: 91, 157
Praying Hands, **SOP**: 75

Dykes, John B.,
"Lead, Kindly Light," **CEW**: 92

Eckhart von Hochheim (Meister Eckhart), **COP**: 139
Eddas, **PPMM**: 155
Eddy, Mary Baker, **CAS**: 296
Edward, King, **PPJC**: 197
Edwards, Jonathan, **RRR**: 231; **PPMM**: 93; **FFF**: 169; **POA**: 394
Ehrhard, Albert,
Der Katholicismus und das zwanzigste Jahrhundert im Lichte der kirchlichen Entwicklung der Neuzeit [Catholicism and the Twentieth Century in Light of the Development of the Church in Modern Times] (1902), **TCS**: 327-328
Elias (OT), **COC**: 99
Elijah (OT), **RRR**: 28; **PPJC**: 65; **SOP**: 75
Eliot, George, **RRA**: 227, 256-257; **WOC**: 127; **COP**: 93; **FFF**: 86, 251; **GHF**: 72
"The Legend of Jubal," **TLTN**: 9-11
Middlemarch; a Study of Provincial Life (1871-1872), **JOG**: 114
Elizabeth I, Queen, **RRR**: 29, 59; **FFF**: 313
Ellicott, Charles John, **MSC**: 117
A Critical and Grammatical Commentary on St. Paul's First Epistle to the Corinthians (1889), **CAS**: 163
Emerson, Ralph Waldo, **POA**: 47, 203; **CAS**: 296
Ephraim (OT), **PPMM**: 131
Epicurus, **JOG**: 56
Erasmus, Desiderius, **RRR**: 126, 231; **PPMM**: 109; **MSC**: 235; **FFF**: 95; **SOP**: 59
Esau (OT), **CEW**: 92
Eucken, Rudolf Christof, **RRR**: viii, 170; **PPMM**: 181, 207; **POA**: 153
Euripides, **COP**: 33
Eusebius of Caesarea, **TCS**: 72
Examiner, **MSC**: 95
Eyck, Hubert van, **COP**: 156
Adoration of the Lamb, **RRA**: 149

Schwenkfeld, Kaspar von Ossig, **FFF**:
 70-71, 81-83, 131
Scott, George Gilbert, **CAS**: 180
Scott-Holland, Canon,
 The City and the Kingdom, **COC**: 40, 42
Seeberg, Reinhold, **PPJC**: viii; **CAS**: 251
Seneca, **TCS**: 73
Servetus, Michael, **POA**: 242
Shaftesbury, Anthony Ashley Cooper,
 RRR: 100; **SCP**: 29
Shakespeare, William, **RRA**: 54, 90-91,
 149, 164, 227-228, 257; **PPMM**: 5, 23,
 227, 244; **PPJC**: 111; **WOC**: 158;
 COP: 33, 73, 90, 93, 108, 239, 253,
 295; **FFF**: 34, 117; **TLTN**: 76; **GHF**:
 84, 92
 As You Like It, **JOG**: 213-214
 Hamlet, **COP**: 264; **JOG**: 213-214;
 CGS-GG: 102; **GHF**: 61
 Henry VIII, **COP**: 198
 King Lear, **JOG**: 213-214; **CGS-GG**:
 102
 Othello, **COP**: 235-236; **JOG**: 213-214
 "64th Sonnet," **RRA**: 29
 The Tempest, **COP**: 96-97; **CGS-GG**:
 102
Shaw, George Bernard, **PPJC**: 248;
 FFF: 189
 *Major Barbara; With an Essay as First
 Aid to Critics* (1907), **FFF**: 280-283
Sheldon, Charles,
 In His Steps, **GHF**: 132
Shelley, Percy Bysshe, **RRA**: x, 48;
 JOG: 135; **GHF**: 56
 "Cenci," **GHF**: 112
Siebeck, Hermann,
 *Zur Religions-philosophie; drei
 Betrachtungen* [The Philosophy of
 Religion: Three Studies] (1907),
 JOG: 224
Sippel, Theodor,
 *"William Dells Programm: Eine
 Lutherischen 'Gemeinschafts-
 bewegung'"* [William Dell's Program:
 A Lutheran Community Movement],
 Zeitschrift für Theologie und Kirche
 Ergänzungsheft 3 (1911), **FFF**: 60

Sippell,
 unidentifed article, *Die Christliche
 Welt* (October 1911), **FFF**: 64
Smith, Adam, **FFF**: 129
Smith, George Adam,
 The Book of Isaiah, 2 vols. (1890),
 WOC: 38
 *The Book of the Twelve Prophets,
 Commonly Called the Minor*, 2 vols.
 (1896-1898), **WOC**: 38
Smith, Herbert A.,
 The Law of Associations, **TCS**: 316
Socini, see Sozzini, Fausto
Socrates, **PPMM**: 34; **MSC**: 55; **PPJC**:
 145; **COP**: 23, 35, 90; **JOG**: 205;
 GHF: 87
Sohm, Rudolph, **CAS**: 65, 67
Solomon (OT), **COP**: 66
Sophocles, **COP**: 28, 32, 33, 253
 Antigone, **COP**: 32
 Oedipus, **COP**: 32
Sozzini, Fausto, **FFF**: 121
Spencer, Herbert, **PPJC**: 193
Spener, Philipp Jakob, **PPJC**: 191
Spinoza, Benedict De, **RRA**: 228; **COP**:
 72, 229; **TLTN**: 50; **CGS-HC**: 19
Spurgeon, Charles Haddon, **COC**: 57
 The Standard, **WOC**: 16
Starbuck, H. D., **POA**: 301, 384
Stead, Herbert, **MSC**: 36
Stonehouse, **MSC**: 36
Story, Dr., **COC**: 22
Strahan, James,
 The Book of Job Interpreted (1913),
 JOG: 224
Strauss, David Friedrich, **RRA**: 173,
 193; **POA**: 125, 267; **JOG**: 209-210
Swedenborg, Emanuel, **CAS**: 304
Swete, Henry Barclay, **TLTN**: 38
Swinburne, Algernon Charles, **RRA**:
 211; **PPJC**: 229; **COP**: 129
 Atalanta in Calydon: A Tragedy
 (1865), **COP**: 253

Tacitus, Cornelius, **MSC**: 61
Tatian, **COP**: 129, 149-150
Tauler, Johann, **COP**: 139

Weiss, Johannes, **PPJC**: 107; **POA**: 65, 86; **CAS**: 153

Weizsäcker, Carl Heinrich von, **WOC**: 244

Wellhausen, Julius, **PPJC**: 112, 263; **JOG**: 213

Wells, [Charles Jeremiah?], **PPJC**: 248

Wernle, Paul, **PPJC**: ix, 30, 148; **CEW**: 165

   The Beginnings of Christianity (1903), **CAS**: 154

Wesley, John, **RRR**: 106; **PPMM**: 17; **PPJC**: 191, 246; **MSC**: 280, 310; **FFF**: 249; **POA**: 262; **TCS**: 26; **CAS**: 29

Westcott, Brooke Foss, **COC**: 53; **JOG**: 94; **CAS**: 165; **CGS-GG**: 120

Whistler, James Abbott McNeil, *Nocturnes*, **COP**: 204

White, Francis,
   The Copies of Severall Letters Contrary to the Opinion of the Present Powers to the Lord Gen. Fairfax and Lieut. Gen. Cromwell (1649), **FFF**: 145

Whitefield, George, **CAR-CR**: 51

Whitman, Walt, **PPMM**: 33; **SCP**: 21

Whittier, John Greenleaf, **CGS-GG**: 121

Wilberforce, William, **MSC**: 192; **POA**: 306

Wilde, Oscar, **COP**: 280
   De Profundis (1905), **COP**: 276

William II, Friedrich Wilhelm Viktor Albert, **CEW**: 2, 18, 57, 70; **JOG**: 119

William III, **COC**: 95; **FFF**: 158, 323

William of Orange, see William III

William the Silent, **FFF**: 135

Williams, John, **MSC**: 40

Williams, Rodger, **FFF**: 149

Winckelmann, Johann Joachim, **COP**: 17

Windelband, Wilhelm, **POA**: 5

Wobbermin, Georg, **PPJC**: 59
   Geschichte und historie in der religions-wissenschaft . . . [Story and History in Religious Studies] (1911), **POA**: 112

Wordsworth, William, **RRA**: 117, 210; **PPMM**: 156, 201; **PPJC**: 67, 127; **WOC**: 16-18; **COP**: 61; **POA**: 119; **JOG**: 135, 214; **SOP**: 43; **TLTN**: 59; **CAR-CR**: 70
   "Carnage is God's Daughter," **JOG**: 178
   "The Excursion," **GHF**: 67
   "She Was a Phantom of Delight," **COP**: 79, 184
   "Wunderhorn," **COP**: 91

Wundt, Wilhelm Max, **PPMM**: 207; **FFF**: 35; **POA**: 173, 329; **TCS**: 153, 155; **JOG**: 51; **TLTN**: 75

Wycliffe, John, **COP**: 146; **FFF**: 78

Zaccheus (NT), **COTC**: 42; **PPJC**: 106

Zahn, Theodor, **PPJC**: ix

Zeno, **JOG**: 56

INDICES FOR SEPARATELY PUBLISHED WORKS

1. Religion in Recent Art

CONTENTS:

2. The Charter of the Church: Six Lectures on the Spiritual Principle of Nonconformity

CONTENTS:

Scripture Index

Old Testament

1 Kings

22:13-14 73

New Testament

Galatians

. . . . 76
. . . . 88

Ephesians

. . . . 47

Index of Names and Cited Works

Abel (OT), 84
Ambrose, 80
Aquinas, Thomas, 87, 92
Augustine of Hippo, 78, 92
Bert, Paul, 101
Bismarck, Otto von, 80
Cain (OT), 84
Calvin, John, 89, 91
Charlemagne, 85, 90
Constantine the Great, 36, 79, 84
Dale, Robert William, 53
Dante Alighieri, 40, 87
Didache, 52
Döllinger, Johann Joseph Ignaz von, 12
Elias (OT), 99
Fairbairn, Dr., 57
Francis of Assisi, 87
Giotto di Bondone, 87
Gregory VII, Pope, 80, 86, 90

Harnack, Adolf von, 53
Hatch, Edwin, 77
Henry IV, King, of Germany, 80, 86
Henry VIII, King of England, 12
Hildebrand, see Gregory VII, Pope
Hume, David, 11
Innocent III, Pope, 86
Jeremiah (OT), 74
Keble, John, 80
King, Edward, 99
Labouchere, Henry Du Pré, 99
Lecky, William Edward Hartpole, 11
Leo XIII, Pope, 90
Luther, Martin, iv, 76, 88, 91
Maclaren, Alexander, 57
Micaiah (OT), 73
Molinari, Gustave de, *Religion* (1894), 24
Moses (OT), 52
Napoleon Bonaparte, 95
Newman, John Henry, 49, 76, 80, 91
Paul, Saint (NT), 18, 39, 75-77
Peter, Saint (NT), 67
Pusey, Edward Bouverie, 80
Rainy, Robert, 55, 57
Robespierre, Maximilien-François-Marie-Isadore de, 95
Robinson, Armitage, 52
Rosebery, Archibald Philip Primrose, 16
Salisbury, Lord, 22
Scott-Holland, Canon, *The City and the Kingdom*, 40, 42
Spurgeon, Charles Haddon, 57
Story, Dr., 22
Theodosius, 80

3. Rome, Reform and Reaction: Four Lectures on the Religious Situation

CONTENTS:

4. Positive Preaching and Modern Mind

CONTENTS:

Scripture Index

Index of Names and Cited Works

5. Missions in State and Church: Sermons and Addresses

CONTENTS:

Index of Names and Cited Works

6. Socialism, the Church and the Poor

CONTENTS:

Scripture Index

Index of Names and Works Cited

7. The Cruciality of the Cross

CONTENTS:

8. The Person and Place of Jesus Christ

CONTENTS:

Index of Names and Cited Works

9. The Work of Christ

CONTENTS:

Scripture Index

Index of Names and Cited Works

10. Christ on Parnassus: Lectures on Art, Ethic, and Theology

CONTENTS:

Scripture Index

Index of Names and Cited Works

11. Faith, Freedom and the Future

CONTENTS:

12. Marriage: Its Ethic and Religion

CONTENTS:

Scripture Index

Index of Names and Cited Works

13. The Principle of Authority in Relation to Certainty, Sanctity and Society

CONTENTS:

Scripture Index

Index of Names and Cited Works

14. Theology in Church and State

CONTENTS:

Scripture Index

Index of Names and Cited Works

15. The Christian Ethic of War

CONTENTS:

Index of Names and Cited Works

16. The Justification of God: Lectures for War-Time on a Christian Theodicy

CONTENTS:

Scripture Index

Index of Names and Cited Works

17. Soul of Prayer

CONTENTS:

Scripture Index

Index of Names and Cited Works

18. The Church and the Sacraments

CONTENTS:

Author's Preface, xv-xvi

Scripture Index

Index of Names and Cited Works

19. This Life and the Next: The Effect on this Life of Faith in Another

CONTENTS:

Scripture Index

Index of Names and Cited Works

20. Congregationalism and Reunion: Two Lectures

CONTENTS:

21. God the Holy Father

CONTENTS:

Scripture Index

Index of Names and Cited Works

22. The Church, the Gospel and Society

CONTENTS:

Scripture Index *(A Holy Church the Moral Guide of Society)*

Old Testament
No references

New Testament
Matthew
11:25 11
25 7

1 Corinthians
13 8

2 Corinthians
5:21 12

1 John
.... 8

Index of Names and Cited Works

Abraham (OT), 53
Athanasius, 20
Calvin, John, 7
Gladden, [Washington], 14
Gore, Charles, 39
Hillel, 16
Luther, Martin, 41, 49-51, 53
MacKennal, Alexander, 13
Moses (OT), 16
Napoleon Bonaparte, 36
Paul, Saint (NT), 19
Plotinus, 19
Ribot, Alexandre-Felix-Joseph, 37
Rousseau, Jean-Jacques, 35
Spinoza, Benedict de, 19

Scripture Index *(The Grace of the Gospel as the Moral Authority of the Church)*

Old Testament
Books of Moses
.... 77

Proverbs
.... 79

New Testament
John
3:16 125

Galatians
2:20 125

Hebrews
.... 81

James
.... 77

Index of Names and Cited Works

Alfred, King, 79
Arnold, Matthew, 100
Browning, Robert, 121
Creighton, Mandell, 119-120
David (OT), 113
Gladstone, William Ewart, 103
Hegel, Georg Wilhelm Friedrich, 97
Lex Mundi, 91
Luther, Martin, 77, 79
Moses (OT), 77, 113
Paul, Saint (NT), 68, 77, 84, 96, 113, 123, 125

TITLE INDEX OF
FORSYTH'S WRITINGS

Book titles appear in capital letters. The numbers following each title refer to numbered entries, not page numbers.

NAME INDEX TO FORSYTH BIBLIOGRAPHY

About the Author

ROBERT BENEDETTO is Associate Librarian at Union Theological Seminary in Virginia. His previous books include *Guide to the Manuscript Collections of the Presbyterian Church, U.S.* (Greenwood Press, 1990). An authority on nineteenth century Presbyterian theology and Reformed missions, his articles have appeared in *American Presbyterians: Journal of Presbyterian History*.

www.ingramcontent.com/pod-product-compliance
Lightning Source LLC
Chambersburg PA
CBHW070444100426
42812CB00004B/1200